<<<<<<<<<<<<<<<<<<<<<<<<<<<<<

CONSTANCE SPRY

A Biography

CONSTANCE SPRY

A Biography

Elizabeth Coxhead

WILLIAM LUSCOMBE PUBLISHER LIMITED
(in association with Mitchell Beazley)

First published in Great Britain by
William Luscombe Publisher Ltd
Artists House
14 Manette Street
London WC1V 5LB
1975

ISBN 0 86002 073 8

Set and printed in Great Britain by
Cox & Wyman Ltd,
London, Fakenham and Reading

<<<<<<<<<<<<<<
CONTENTS

≪≪≪≪≪≪≪≪≪≪≪≪≪≪≪≪≪≪≪≪≪≪≪≪≪≪≪≪≪
ACKNOWLEDGMENTS

This book would not have been possible without the help of Constance Spry's friends and colleagues, who gave me most generously of their time and reminiscences.

I am particularly indebted to Miss Effie Barker, Lady Barnett, Dr Kate Barratt, Lord Bernstein, Mme Bourdillon, Mrs Buckingham, Mrs Lily Cook, Miss Melora Cumings, Mrs Christine Dickie, Mrs Ducker, Lord and Lady Eccles, Mr Gilbert Fletcher, Mr Lynton Fletcher, Mrs Marjorie Fletcher, Mr George Foss, Miss Eva Hackett, Mr Roy Hay, Miss Daphne Holden, Miss Rosemary Hume, Mrs Robert Lovett, Mrs Sheila Macqueen, Mrs McPherson, Lady Maufe, Mrs Robbins Milbank, Mr Beverley Nichols, Mr Harold Piercy, Mrs Mary Pope, Lady Portarlington, Mrs Edmund Rich, Mrs Patricia Easterbrook Roberts, Mrs Evelyn Russell, Mrs Cameron Smail, Mrs H. E. Spry, Mr Victor Stiebel, Mrs John Stuart, Mr Graham Thomas, Miss Florence Thurston, Miss Marjorie Towers, Mr and Mrs Walter Trower, Mr Basil Unite.

Mr R. E. Marston and his staff at the Central Library, Derby, unearthed for me facts about the Fletcher family in their Derby days. The late Marjorie, Lady Pentland, and the Superintendant of Peamount Hospital, Newcastle, County Dublin, made available to me material relevant to Lady Aberdeen's activities in Ireland. An appeal by Miss Jacqueline Rose of the *Hackney Gazette* put me in touch with people who had been pupils of Homerton Day Continuation School under the headship of Constance Marr. Mr Keith Henderson gave me his reminiscences of his friend Norman Wilkinson 'of Four Oaks'.

Both Author and Publisher wish to thank the following for permission to reproduce the photographs as here indicated.

1, *A.A.I.P.*, Derby; 4, *Radio Times Hulton Picture Library*; 2, 3, 7, 8, 9, 10, 11, 12, 13, 14 and 15, *Popperton*; 5, *Press Association Ltd*; 6, *P. A. Reuter Photos Ltd*; 16 and 17, *Helen Robbins Milbank*.

PREAMBLE

The masculine values, Virginia Woolf complained, prevail. Football and sport are important, fashion is trivial. A scene laid on a battlefield has more significance than a scene laid in a shop. Mrs Woolf was writing a feminist tract, and it would be more just to say that these values reflect our long climb, with frequent backslidings, out of barbarism and into civilization. Man appreciates beauty and comfort quite as much as woman, and has hitherto been their principal creator. But the slant is still the same as when she wrote in 1929 – reinforced by our having endured far wider and more dreadful battlefields in the meantime. The importance of the major artists is grudgingly conceded in the footnotes to history. The importance of the applied artists, the designers and decorators and craftsmen, is virtually ignored.

Yet it is they who principally influence our appearance, our surroundings, our behaviour. Much of their work is trivial, no doubt. But where they are of sufficient stature, and their creations are backed by a valid philosophy of life, the results are not trivial, but extraordinarily persistent. Robert Adam means more to us now than Robert Walpole, William Morris than William Gladstone. They altered the way people looked at things; they left on their age a mark which persists into our own. And so, I make bold to prophesy, it will prove with Constance Spry.

Her name is chiefly, and rightly, associated with the arrangement of flowers; as her brother Gilbert has observed with modest pride, it isn't everyone who invents a brand-new art. But she was above all an educator, as her father was before her, and flower-arrangement was one of several means she used to this end. She was born into a poor Victorian home, brought up in increasingly lavish Edwardian ones, and reacted equally against the drabness of the first and the pretentiousness of the second. She bridged the gap between Edwardian gracious living – essentially vulgar because based on the possession of money and on the labour of underpaid servants – and that of our own age, where the graciousness, if any, must be supplied by ourselves.

She took little from the settings of her youth except a liking for cosy clutter; with her, however, always exquisitely controlled. Her inspirations came from further back, from the Dutch and Flemish flower paintings of the seventeenth century, the English and French furniture and ornaments of the eighteenth. But she was no antiquarian; what she demonstrated was the creative use of beautiful things out of the past, and the reinterpretation of old styles in contemporary terms.

Admittedly, the style she evolved has little in common with the austerities of Le Corbusier or *le style scandinave,* which are supposed to express the decorative needs of the machine age. But do they? The craving for pattern and elaboration lies very deep in human nature and is found in almost all primitive art; the art evolved by the ancestors of these self-same Scandinavians is a case in point. And only recently, our young designers joyously rediscovered the work of Morris, which in its turn embodied oriental motifs of extreme antiquity.

What the machine age has chiefly landed us with is a load of disposable rubbish; this, as is so often and justly said, is the age of waste. Much of the rubbish is pleasant in design, but its built-in obsolescence ensures that it will give no lasting pleasure to its possessor. And once again, this fails to satisfy a human craving. Hence the reaction, the frantic and often pathetic searching in junkshops for some one object made of real materials, into the fashioning of which somebody once put real craftsmanship. Constance Spry, herself an early and brilliantly successful junkshop frequenter, knew that in the long run this was no solution. She campaigned for better objects within the range of everyone's purse, though this side of her teaching has not, so far, borne much fruit, and she taught improvisation

‹‹‹

1. *Below inset:* Constance Fletcher's birthplace,
No. 58 Warner Street, Derby.

2. *Below:* Constance Spry's last home, Winkfield Place, near Windsor.

3. *Above:* Placing the vital first branch.

4. *Below:* Judging at an early flower-arrangement show, with Mrs. Mary Pope.

with objects like country baskets, wooden bowls, baking-tins, that are available to all.

Like most applied artists, she had to rely on rich patrons of taste and discrimination to make her ideas known. She is therefore still associated in people's minds with luxury, with the decoration of the grand ballroom or the fashionable wedding church. But the first half of her working life was spent among the really poor, and she never forgot their hunger for beauty, their touching appreciation of any scrap that came their way. 'Flowers are for everyone,' she insisted time and time again, and by 'flowers' she meant more than just the contents of a vase. Hence her great hopes at the start of the flower-club movement, her intense pride in being given charge of the flowers on the route of the Coronation procession, which thousands would enjoy.

She lived long enough to see the extreme poverty of her youth abolished, and the spread of a relative affluence among large sections of the working people. We certainly have a long way to go before her standards of beauty and civilized living prevail, but lack of taste, that is to say, of education, is now a bigger obstacle than lack of means. For one always comes back to education, with Constance Spry. She was a teacher, by heredity and instinct, by book and lecture, by precept and example. Of course some details of her teaching have dated, but that does not signify. Its effect and aim can still be summarized as they were by one of her pupils in London's East End. 'She made us feel alive, and free.'

1. CONSTANCE FLETCHER

It was generally supposed, by those who met her after she was famous, that Constance Spry was Irish, and tribute was often paid to her typically Irish warmth and vivacity. This agreeable assumption she was at no great pains to contradict. Indeed, in the opening pages of *A Garden Notebook*, she harks back to 'the old Irish garden of my childhood,' telling us how she saved her Saturday penny to buy seeds, and how, when tidied for the afternoon, she hid in a bush by the drive, hoping to salvage droppings for her own little plot when the carriages bringing callers should arrive, and how Authority swooped and punished her, and made her ashamed ... All of which suggests a tiny tot brought up in starchy splendour, not a young lady who was half-way through her high school career before ever she set foot on Irish soil.

Well, she is not on oath, not telling her life story, merely enlivening a book about gardening. What she has to say is true in its essence, though not accurate as to time and place. It corresponds with what we have come to call the Image. She and her father *were* Irish in temperament and outlook, and as nothing is known about their forbears, they may possibly have had Irish blood. It is certain that George Fletcher was one of the very few English administrators who came to be accepted by the Irish as one of themselves.

From jottings – all too brief, alas – which Constance made towards the end of her life, perhaps with an autobiography in mind, it is clear that she would not in fact have disowned her very humble origins in the back streets of Derby. She took a

5

pride in her father's meteoric rise from such small beginnings, as she did in all the achievements of his career.

There are many worse places to be born in than Derby. Of the Midland industrial towns, it is by far the most attractive. One goes north through a street of Georgian houses which might grace a cathedral close, and a short way farther on lies the glorious country of the Peak. But it was from the wrong side of the tracks that the Fletcher children came, from the mean little streets of red-brick terraced houses round the railway station. At Number 58 Warner Street, on the 5th of December 1886, Constance was born, the first child and only girl of George Fletcher and his wife Henrietta Maria, formerly Clark.

George Fletcher had left school at fourteen, started work as a printer's devil, then become a telegraphist with the Midland Railway Company, getting himself a qualification in electrical engineering through night classes; but his positively Renascence hunger for universal knowledge was not to be satisfied with that. He acquired a smattering of the other basic sciences at the Derby Technical School, and at the same time he attended courses in arts subjects run by lecturers from Cambridge. Thus, in 1885 he enrolled for 'Literary Masterpieces' and 'Plant Life'; in 1886 for 'Studies in the History of Art'; in 1887, for 'The Forces of Nature' and 'Astronomy'; in 1888 for 'Sound and Music'. In all these subjects he acquired certificates of distinction; no other student came anywhere near him. In what small free time he can have had left, he painted in water-colour and wrote poetry. One is tempted to say, an artist *manqué*; but it is clear that the artist in him was to find fulfilment in becoming an educator, and passing on in his turn the sense of joy and liberation that learning had brought to him.

Tall and fair, handsome and genial, he chose as wife a woman physically and in every other respect his opposite, a little, dark, elegant person, pretty and sharp-tongued. She was two years older than he was, and came of small gentlefolk; she believed herself to have come down in the world by marrying him. She had a natural good taste and feeling for fine objects, appreciated Georgian mahogany long before it came back into fashion, and collected it as soon as she could. Her refinement must have been one of her attractions for him, and certainly her fierce social ambition helped his rise. But she was not a woman fitted to bring happiness, either to her husband, or to her children, or to herself.

It is difficult to be fair to Etty Fletcher; her particular brand of snobbery has gone out of fashion, though doubtless it still lurks in the undergrowth. But one can have more sympathy with her after seeing 58 Warner Street and 53 Sale Street, the grim little terraced houses, with the merest vestige of back yard, in which she spent her first married years. Smoke abatement at least renders this part of Derby fresh and clean today, but in the days when every household burned raw coal, it must have been grimy also. One can understand how passionately she longed to leave it, how she was determined not to let her children mix with the others of the neighbourhood, how she worked to keep them neat and clean and always on show. And whatever her faith in her husband's gifts, she had no guarantee that the family would ever escape. By the time they did, the harm was done.

There is evidence that she did try to share his interests, and it can't have been easy, with all that toil, and a pregnancy every other year. She joined the Derby University Students' Association, though there is no record of what classes she attended. When George became its vice-president, she sat on the committee. She accompanied him on geologizing trips to the Peak, and heard him subsequently read papers to the Derbyshire Archaeological and Natural History Society. And indeed, it was his mania for learning that brought her the order of release. His instructors at the Technical College felt that he was wasted as a railway telegraphist, and shortly after Constance's birth he was invited to join its staff. By 1891 he was its Headmaster and principal science teacher, at a salary of £200 a year.

That was a middle-class income in the 1890s, and the Fletchers – by now there were five of them – could move into a middle-class house, 59 Wilson Street, a mile nearer the centre of the town. This was the first home Constance could consciously remember, and her memories were not cheerful ones. For although three-storey, and roomy, it was still only a terrace house, with a few shrubs in front and a yard behind, and round it stretched more red brick, giving the endless boring walks of which her childhood seemed full, her little legs trotting beside the giant stride of her mother, who pushed Arnold and baby Kenneth in the pram.

Some of the surrounding houses had gardens, however, and for the first time the child found 'a heady excitement in the few flowers that came my way.' There was still no servant, but an old Derbyshire countrywoman was sometimes hired to take the brood for walks, and she told them of a red rose so dark as to be almost black. Always they looked for it, never found it, and at last lost faith in the old body; but half a lifetime later, Constance found the French moss-rose *Nuits de Young*, introduced into Britain in 1851, and it came to her that the story might have been true.

Relations between mother and daughter were difficult from the start. The eldest, and her father's darling, Constance was the rival, the other woman. Of a temperament that throve on praise and encouragement, she received instead a diet of snubs, and these so rankled that when, as a middle-aged woman, she came to write books on flower arrangement, out the snubs tumbled – irrelevant, as often as not, but with their sting still fresh. 'Authority', as Etty always figures in her books, can do no right; the feeling is one of positive hate.

Two photographs of Constance survive from Derby days, and they suggest a tough little person, whom the snubs might wound but could never cow. In one, she is crowing with glee, and this is how she would greet the adored father, with his life-enhancing enthusiasm and humour. The other shows a rock-like obstinacy, and this would be the face her mother saw.

To herself, she seemed to be entirely her father's child. But of course we inherit from both parents, and genius, as often as not, seems to need the clash of uncongenial personalities for its production. It was from her mother that Constance had her vivacity, her quickness (but never unkindness) of tongue, her deft fingers, her flair for unearthing beautiful objects, her eye that missed nothing. And although, as she grew up, she seemed to have in large measure George's open, sunny optimism, there was a darker element of taut nerves that came from Etty, and was lying in wait to trap her in later life.

George, at all events, had good reason for his optimism; the element of luck which even the highest abilities require was never to fail him in his career. The chief of the Department of Science at the Board of Education in London was another brilliant son of Derby, Sir William Abney. The successes which the young headmaster, with no more than night-school training, was achieving in the teaching of science in his home town were brought to his notice. In 1894 George found himself promoted to the inspectorate, with responsibility for science teaching in a section of the West Country based in Plymouth. The Fletcher family left Derby, never to return.

The move to Plymouth was the first great escape for Constance, the first complete revelation of beauty. Writing long afterwards,* she describes 'the almost delirious happiness, remembered to this day, that was mine when I was made free of the wild flowers of the West Country lanes and fields.' There were white violets on Mount Edgecumbe, there were hart's tongue ferns on the banks of the lanes. And there was a gentleman's house with a proper garden, in which, no doubt, the incident of the manure took place.

The family were two years in Plymouth, where another brother, Donald, was added to the strength. Then George Fletcher received further promotion, being put in charge of science inspection for the whole of the Midland division, and they travelled back again, but this time to a house in the pleasant and prosperous Birmingham suburb of Moseley, where Gilbert was born. Only Lynton, the baby of the family, was to be born in Ireland, and make Constance's row of tall handsome brothers complete.

For her, it was good-bye to the idyll of running wild in flowery lanes. She was now of high-school age, and started her serious education at King Edward's School, Birmingham; and the education of a Fletcher child was serious indeed. She recalls with distaste the endless lessons, the depressing schoolrooms, the ugly clothes. She was not academically minded, but she worked hard to please her father, and his own comment and inspiration could always make the homework worth doing.

* *Simple Flowers*, page 1.

She might well have expected to complete her schooldays here, but they were to be interrupted once again. At the turn of the century, an exciting new prospect opened up before English experts in technical education – that of tilling a virgin field, and bringing the same enlightenment to Ireland.

Shamefully slow and backward though the spread of technical education among the English working-classes had been, in Ireland provision for it was non-existent, until a group of Irish Members of Parliament, headed by Horace Plunkett, who had already organized a system of co-operative creameries among the Irish peasantry, forced the Government at Westminster to pass an Irish Agriculture and Technical Instruction Bill. Funds were voted, and a department of instruction in these subjects was officially opened in April 1900, with Plunkett as its vice-president, and his friend T. P. Gill, the brilliant journalist and nationalist politician, as its secretary. They at once set about recruiting staff, and naturally looked to England, where the experience was. Equally naturally, this infuriated Irishmen, who perceived well-paid new appointments going to the hated oppressor. The feeling aroused is said to have cost Plunkett his seat at the next election. It did not matter to him greatly. He had got his way, and he was a wealthy aristocrat, who regarded personal aggrandizement with a fine and noble disdain.

Gill accordingly came over on what we would now call a milk-round. His choice for the all-important post of Assistant Secretary in charge of the new Department's technical education side fell on Robert Blair, already marked out as one of the coming men in education. And either Blair, or perhaps Abney, recommended George Fletcher as chief inspector of technical education, the post immediately next to Blair's. It took some time to get the personnel recruited and make the new department more than just an address, but Blair was at his new desk by May of 1901, and by the autumn, George Fletcher was at his.

It was work after their hearts. Successive English administrators had pronounced the Irish peasantry uneducable; Blair and Fletcher had no difficulty in proving this untrue. Young Irishmen were just as keen as their English counterparts to acquire skills which would take them off the potato patch and into work-shop or factory, or which would at any rate make the potato patch more repaying. The prejudice against English officials did not extend into the countryside; they were welcome wherever they went.

It had all to be done from scratch, with sketchy funds, and a constant harrying of the Treasury for more. Committees of technical instruction were formed under all the local authorities in the country, and Fletcher visited them all, many of them several times. 'Education cannot succeed without the interest and goodwill of the country as a whole,' he wrote in one of his early reports. They had to find instructors, which in the first instance meant taking teachers out of the primary schools and giving them crash courses in carpentry, metalwork or whatever it might be, 'not claimed as a perfect method but the only one possible,' Fletcher admitted. They had to find buildings, and even with a grant from the Department there was seldom money to erect new ones, but miracles of adaptation were performed on disused fever hospitals, jails, Protestant chapels, (in the country, Protestantism was rapidly losing out to the dominant religion). One little town adapted a water tower, another even contrived its technical school inside a disused water tank. Domestic science schools were started for the girls; they did not amount to much more than training for domestic service, but at any rate their pupils would be better domestic servants, and, one hopes, earn better wages, than those who came to the Big House straight out of the bog.

There was great flexibility, allowing schools to adapt their curricula to local requirements; 'there is in consequence a refreshing diversity among the Technical Schools,' Fletcher reported. Genial and gay, with a fund of good stories, he never made the mistake of talking down to them, as an administrator with a public-school background might have done. He was a boy from the back streets, who had come up from small beginnings, just as they were doing, and he knew how to inspire them with confidence. The education so hardly won in the night-schools of Derby was the best possible preparation for this job.

. . . . . .

The Fletchers' first Irish home, Dawson Court, Blackrock, was perhaps the most attractive of their wandering career; a rambling old house off Mount Merrion Avenue, with the big walled garden and the blue ceanothus hedge Constance remembered so lovingly – though, when she first saw them, she was well past the age when Mrs Fletcher would have allowed dirtying of hands and pinafores. In any case, the pressure of lessons was as relentless as ever. She was entered at Alexandra School, the only possible choice for a man of Fletcher's views. It offered the best education a girl could get in Ireland – as, indeed, it still does.

Alexandra College had been founded in 1866, in emulation of the pioneer Queen's College in London, to provide higher education for girls of ability; most of the lectures were given by Trinity College professors, though Trinity would not admit the students to degrees. The School was started in 1881, to prepare for admission to the College. The Heads at the time of George Fletcher's arrival were two remarkable women, Miss Isabella Mulvaney at the School and Miss H. M. White at the College; a year or two later Trinity was to give them both honorary doctorates. He at once formed personal friendships with them, and indeed, thought so highly of Dr Mulvaney that when his two youngest sons reached prep-school age, he persuaded her to admit first one and then the other, each with a companion to keep him in countenance. Accordingly, Gilbert and Lynton Fletcher and their friends can boast of being the only four boys educated at Alexandra. Needless to say, they were petted and indulged. Lynton, hauled before Dr Mulvaney for some misdemeanour, remembers that he was first rebuked in due form; then he and she sloped off together, leaving the school to get on without them, and spent the rest of the afternoon at the Dublin Zoo.

Constance was probably happier at Alexandra than she had been in Birmingham. She always loved Ireland and felt at home there, and when she could escape from her mother's chilling shadow, she easily made friends. But her academic record continued to be undistinguished; she felt she was a disappointment to her father, and grew much discouraged. She knew herself to have abilities, yet no one seemed to value them or find an outlet for them. She had a mind rich in the fascinating information he brought home and in the poetry he so much valued, but she could get nothing down on paper. From these years date her dislike and distrust of examinations, and indeed, of competition in any form.

George Fletcher saw some facet of his many talents in each of his children, and apart from Kenneth, who turned out an amiable rolling stone, he was justified. Arnold became a brilliant research geologist under the famous Professor Joly at Trinity. Donald was a medical student of great promise. Gilbert had a distinguished career in colonial administration, and Lynton, inheriting George's electrical abilities, became a chief sound engineer with the BBC. Constance, it seemed plain to her father, was the artist of the family, and once again his educator's instinct guided him correctly. What he could not discover was the form her artistic gift was to take.

He saw that she was already, as she says, 'preoccupied with flowers and colour'; he arranged for her to have drawing lessons. They were a complete failure. Her hands were marvellously dextrous with the needle or in any other household task, but she could not draw a line, not then or ever. (In her later professional life she got over the difficulty by always having someone around who could draw for her). What was worse, the lessons in taste and design which the instructor was trying to impart fell on deaf ears. The Art Nouveau re-interpretation of Celtic patterns had become a dogma of the Irish Renascence, and she was invited to copy a sinuous frieze of convolvulus. 'I don't like flowers made to do that,' she had the impertinence to remark, and so, 'Father's artist *manqué* was in the dog-house.'*

Still hopeful, he insisted that she study the reproductions in *The Studio*, to which he was a subscriber. She turned the pages only 'dutifully', she tells us, though much must have sunk into her subconscious; not the texture and techniques of paint, but outline, particularly the outline of the great flower painters. But one day she was jolted into real enthusiasm by a highly stylized painting of Richard II holding the Red Rose of

---

* *Favourite Flowers*, page 28.

Lancaster; at the King's feet a parterre of exquisite and strange flowers, flaked pinks, striped and spotted roses. Many years afterwards she was to meet the artist, who would profoundly influence her work.*

The Fletcher luck held. In 1904 Blair was offered, and of course accepted, one of the key posts in English education, that of Education Officer to the London County Council. George Fletcher stepped into his shoes, becoming Assistant Secretary to the Department and head of its technical instruction; in fact, under the liberal and sympathetic general direction of Gill, the boss of his own show. Popular from the start, he was now a figure of real importance in Dublin, and his section's influence was so widespread and benevolent that it became known as The Department *tout court,* as though the Civil Service comprised no other. When Arnold and Donald got into some minor scrape with the police, and it was discovered that they were the sons of 'Mr Fletcher of The Department', they were smilingly let go.

George needed to be nearer his office in Leeson Street, and the family moved once again, to 53 Pembroke Road, one of those semi-detached, but vast, Dublin Georgian houses which are mansions in themselves. It had thirteen separate staircases, Lynton remembers, and his mother now commanded a staff of five servants. Mrs Fletcher was in her glory, her ambition to become a leading Dublin hostess could be fulfilled. And as such she is still remembered, with real liking. Her parties were beautifully done, and successful; she herself had charm of manner and a flair for collecting interesting people; friendships, and matches, were made in her drawing-room. What the visitors could not know was the unhappy state of tension that prevailed behind the scenes.

George, though naturally hospitable, would have been content with a less lavish display. Although his salary was much increased, he was nevertheless often worried by her extravagance. The children felt themselves to be always on show; they were made to recite, sing, or play the violin. The two little boys were invited into school friends' homes in the free and

* *Summer and Autumn Flowers,* page 66.

14

easy Irish style, but they would never invite their friends back, because if they did, their mother made an occasion of it, with special food and best behaviour. The underlying pathos of her situation is apparent. Though she disliked her daughter, she was genuinely fond and proud of her sons, but quite unable to understand their nature and needs.

Arnold and Donald, the inseparables, escaped from her very effectively by finding themselves a hideout in the Wicklow hills, a semi-derelict cottage reached only on foot, which they named 'Araby', and to which they resorted on bicycles at week-ends. (In later years their father made a road to it and rebuilt it as a holiday house.) And Constance, who loved them dearly, longed to go too, but there could be no question of that. She loved cooking, and would worm her way into the kitchen to bake them cakes and pasties, but even this was frowned upon. She was being groomed by her mother for fine-ladyhood, and by her father for a serious career.

She had failed to show talent as an artist, but she was full of goodwill and wished to be of use in the world. For her sixteenth birthday treat, she asked to have a Dublin slum famliy at 53 Pembroke Road for the day. (They were so filthy that they had to be bathed on arrival; the eldest boy indignantly refused to be bathed by the young lady of the house, but finally consented to the ministrations of a housemaid). Some form of social work seemed indicated. Fletcher himself was deeply perturbed by the poor state of health he had found among young people when he went round the technical schools, and among his many other preoccupations, he had found time to give lectures on simple hygiene and sanitation. In England, local authorities were already beginning to employ women health lecturers, who toured clubs and factories and the upper forms of schools; he determined that this was what Constance should become.

It is unlikely that she was drawn to medicine for its own sake. In later life, she showed an absolute dread of illness, her own or other people's, and a profound distrust of doctors. But she wanted to work with people, already realizing that she had her father's gift for handling them and persuading them to do things, and she seemed to have no alternative bent. And so, though a long and arduous course of training lay ahead of her, she agreed.

She moved up into the College, coming under Dr White, who took a great liking to her. Dr White, among other innovations, had got horticulture opened as a career for educated girls. She is said to have taken a jaunting car up to Glasnevin Gardens, and sat in the Director's office, refusing to go away until he agreed to lay her request for the admission of women pupils before the Council. And this would probably have been far more to Constance's taste, but neither parent would have countenanced it.

A fellow-student at Alexandra College remembers Constance as a lively girl, much more fashionable than the general run, most of her clothes being made by herself. It was a period of wide-brimmed, shallow-crowned picture hats, and most of her allowance went on these; all through her life she carried a liking for this millinery style. She was not as pretty as her mother, her features being a trifle too sharp, but she was piquant, bubbling with ideas, and very good fun. It is also remembered that she was beginning to do original flower arrangements, and that the mothers of several students would invite her to do them for dinner parties; once she opened out tulips to make them look like waterlilies, a startling innovation. It was part of her duty to do the flowers for dinner-parties at home, but here Mrs Fletcher was not allowing any innovations; they had to be the rigidly conventional decoration of epergnes filled with carnations and fern, and the results, in Constance's own opinion, were 'merely grotesque'.

In her year at the College she studied hygiene and physiology, with lessons in physics from her father, and attended lectures in sanitation given by the Professor of Public Health, Antony Roche. Then followed six months' training in district nursing at St. Lawrence's Home for Jubilee Nurses, and a summer course of instruction in food analysis at the Cecilian Street Medical School, against which she put the ominous word 'starvation' – it was certainly a common cause of ill-health in the Dublin of 1905.

It was then decided to send her to London, so that she could take the full course for health lecturers instituted by the National

Health Society. This covered much the same ground, with the addition of courses on bacteriology and on 'The Art of Lecturing', at Kings College, a course on Local Government at the London School of Economics, and a course of instruction for sanitary inspectors at the Royal Sanitary Institute.

Such a programme can hardly have left much time for enjoying metropolitan amusements, and her address, Hopkinson House, a woman students' hostel in Vauxhall Bridge Road, suggests a conventual existence, as does a story she was fond of telling against herself. As she waited one day at a bus stop, a man accosted her with the usual gambit: 'Haven't we met before?' Little Miss Fletcher, known to everyone in Dublin as the daughter of The Department, replied in all innocence: 'Oh, you must be a friend of my father –' and overcome, the would-be seducer fled.

Nothing else seems to have remained in her memory of the Hopkinson House days except her friendship with an art student named Florence Standfast, who will reappear.

In 1907 she secured her first post, no doubt through the helpful influence of her father's former chief, Blair, now Sir Robert. She was appointed assistant lecturer under the London County Council, and did the demonstrating at first-aid and home nursing lectures given by doctors; she quickly graduated to become an independent lecturer herself. In January of 1908, she applied to the Essex Education Committee, for the post of woman health lecturer in elementary schools throughout the county, and it is from her elaborately printed application and testimonials that I take these details of her training.

Whether she was offered the post has not transpired; she may have been considered too young; at all events, she did not take it. Instead, she was recalled to Dublin by her father. He had found her a more exciting opening, nearer home.

The Earl and Countess of Aberdeen had returned to the Viceregal Lodge for their second term of office in February of 1906. Their first had been a mere eighteen months, in 1886–7, but it was long enough to arouse in this high-minded Scottish couple a passionate love of Ireland, and an equally passionate determination to alleviate Irish poverty and distress. Ishbel

Aberdeen started her Irish Industries Association, which was almost 'The Department' in little, for it promoted a small-holding economy of rabbit-keeping and poultry, as well as encouraging lace-making, tweed-weaving and the other traditional crafts. It was a bitter blow when the fall of the Liberal Government brought their appointment to an end, and even a subsequent Governor-generalship of Canada was not a consolation.

But Lady Aberdeen did not let her interest in her brainchild die because her husband was no longer the Lord Lieutenant. She constantly made the tedious journey from her home near Aberdeen to Dublin for meetings of the Association, though tactfully allowing the Conservative Lady-Lieutenant to appear as figure-head. She used her husband's capital to get shops for the crafts opened in Dublin and in London; and she used Andrew Carnegie's millions as backing for a complete Irish village at the first World's Fair, which was held in Chicago in 1893. Weavers and metalworkers were brought over, pretty colleens from the farthest corners of Kerry, Connemara and Donegal were chosen to spin, sing, make butter and dance jigs. There were fifteen cottages grouped round a village green, with a Celtic cross, and a replica of Blarney Castle; it will be seen that Her Ladyship had a flair for publicity far ahead of her time. The Irish–American heart was touched, visitors thronged the exhibit, and far from costing the guarantors anything, it showed in the six months of the Fair a profit of £50,000. And all this, together with thousands of pounds' worth of orders, flowed back into Irish homes.

Returning to the official position and the increase of influence that went with it, Lady Aberdeen was naturally a warm friend to 'The Department', which was doing with Government money what she had tried to do with merely voluntary funds. Soon she was a warm personal friend to George Fletcher also. In aims and in personality they were rather alike – both large and genial, with a sunny charm of manner masking a steely determination. But he was the better of the two at conciliating the opposition; she, born and bred a great lady, was a trifle too apt to brush it aside.

She announced an Irish Lace Ball for the coming viceregal

5. *Above:* By the lake at Winkfield.

6. *Below:* Coming through her borders of 'old' roses. Her collection was the most extensive of any gardener in Britain.

season, which would keep all the lacemakers busy; then she turned her attention to health. Dublin's infant mortality figures were the worst in Europe, and the countryside was not much better. Tuberculosis ravaged whole families in the tiny cramped cottages, and as she continually stressed, its greatest incidence was between the ages of fifteen and thirty-five – the same age-group from which the great drain by emigration came.

She invited all women of goodwill to help her, but not under a negative banner; they were not to be against infant mortality or T.B., but for positive health. The Women's National Health Association of Ireland was inaugurated in March of 1907. The programme aimed to secure district nurses for every community, to set up creches (called mother-and-baby clubs) and pure-milk depots, to start penny dinners in schools and health lectures for schoolchildren, to encourage the keeping of goats and the growing of vegetables, to get windows opened in the cottages and tenements (many of them proved to have been nailed up for forty years).

There was an international exhibition in Dublin that summer, and Lady Aberdeen persuaded the organizers to give her free space for an exhibit of the W N H A. Representatives of local authorities, clergy and wellwishers crowded in, both to the display itself and to the lectures accompanying it. All wanted a visit from display and lecturer, and the requests were met, provided the lecturer could be given hospitality and a hall put at her disposal. The display went on a popular progress through the country, new branches of the Association being formed wherever it went; and if it were within reasonable distance of Dublin, Her Excellency often accompanied it in person, proving a first-class draw.

To tour the remote districts of the far west, where conditions were among the worst and where there was little accommodation for travellers, she equipped at her own expense a horse-drawn caravan, which she named 'Eire' – the first time such a vehicle had been used for publicity in the United Kingdom. It was staffed by an Irish-speaking doctor, a cookery demonstrator and a driver, and the meetings were held in schoolhouses or even in the open. Audiences loved it; many of them walked ten and twelve miles over the mountains, stood for two hours to hear talks enlivened with music and dancing, and then were loath to go home.

The Association grew so rapidly that it became evident there must be some paid staff. A full-time lecturer could take most of the burden off doctors and nurses who had been giving their services free. And whom could Lady Aberdeen have found more suitable, than the daughter of her new friend George Fletcher, who had been thoroughly trained with just this sort of work in view, and was already doing it in London?

So Constance came back to 53 Pembroke Road, but no longer as her mother's dogsbody and butt. She was now an independent young woman with an important career, which took her away from home, sometimes for weeks together. And she presently stood in an almost daughterly relationship to the Vicereine, finding there the appreciation and encouragement that had been lacking at home.

But Etty Fletcher, too, seems to have softened considerably in these years of social flowering. Her family had arrived; they had the entrée to Viceregal Lodge; even she could feel that George and Constance were doing her credit. Lynton remembers the equerries, spendid in helmet and spurs, sitting on their horses in the drive. They were not allowed to dismount, so they waited for someone to come out and take a letter or an invitation from Her Excellency, while all the neighbours saw.

To her many other burdens, Lady Aberdeen now added that of magazine editor. *Slainte*, Irish for 'health', a monthly, made its bow in January of 1909, with pretty Mary-blue covers, nice large print and a few illustrations, price a penny. After her exhausting viceregal day, Lady Aberdeen must have sat up far into the night, toiling over proofs. The files of the paper, preserved among the archives of Peamount Hospital, form a page of Irish social history which has, I think, been overlooked. From them we can get a picture of the Women's National Health Association's endeavours and achievements, and of Miss Constance Fletcher's part in them.

She was ruthlessly overworked; so were all the other young women associated with Lady Aberdeen. They none of them minded. They were eager and idealistic; she made them feel that they were doing something of enormous importance, and they knew that she worked even harder herself. 'Her Ex', as they affectionately called her behind her back, was the kindest of task-mistresses. Her method was always, like George Fletcher's, that of encouragement and praise. Herself a naturally shy woman, she had conquered her diffidence and inspired others to do the same; and when the team returned to Dublin from their gruelling lecture rounds, she saw to it that they shared in the gaieties and good things Viceregal Lodge had to offer. In all this, she set a pattern for the future Constance Spry.

There was at first only one fulltime paid lecturer, Constance, and one part-timer, the rest being still unpaid volunteers. Naturally, Constance was the hardest-worked; she records ninety-five lectures in one autumn season. She often spoke three times a day, to housewives in the morning, to school-children in the afternoon, and in the evening a lecture to which the men turned up in gratifyingly large numbers. *Slainte* reports in its second issue that 'Miss Constance Fletcher's services are in constant request,' and in the April number, the secretary of the Association's Wexford branch writes: 'Miss Constance Fletcher is concluding a course of eight lectures, every one of which has been closely followed by highly interested and attentive audiences. Her practical demonstrations, her lucid descriptions, and above all her charm of manner, have quite fascinated her audiences, and even the most unlearned can carry away something worth remembering. Her lectures on First Aid to the Injured, and on Home Nursing, have been specially popular, numbers of people remaining behind at her invitation to learn by actual practice upon volunteer patients.'

Here again we recognise ingredients of her future technique – charm, lucidity, an audience encouraged to participate. There was elegance too, for Lady Aberdeen wisely did not put her lecturers into uniform, and Constance with her big hats brought a sight of Dublin fashion to the little provincial towns. Her touch with the children was particularly good; she set them to writing essays, which she would judge on her next time round. That her teaching had sunk in was proved by such gems as one small girl's advocacy of mother's milk in preference to cow's for babies, 'because the cat can't get at it.'

In July 1909, we learn from *Slainte*, Constance is chief lecturer at an Infant Mortality Campaign run by Lady Aberdeen in Dublin. She spends her August 'holidays' visiting children's hospitals and clinics in London and Liverpool. By October she heads a team of four lecturers, so rapidly has the movement grown.

Today, when advances in medicine have almost wiped out tuberculosis, the methods advocated by the Women's National Health Association appear to us pathetically inadequate. It must have seemed a hopeless task urging cleanliness when the majority of working-class dwellings had no piped water or sanitation, better food when there was no money to buy it, and isolation of the tubercular person when the family lived, as many did both in and out of Dublin, six to a room.

But Lady Aberdeen had behind her a fund of goodwill. She had contrived to cut right across those antagonisms of race and religion that have bedevilled so many attempts at Irish reform. Parish priests and nuns were among her warmest supporters. She secured a Government grant for 'halfpenny dinners' in schools, the meals being provided and cooked by the local branch of the Association, and Constance is 'delighted to see the halfpenny dinner in progress, and to hear the nuns say how much easier it is to teach the children.' Pending the opening of a central tuberculosis hospital, two disused coastguard stations were offered to Lady Aberdeen by her brother, then First Lord of the Admiralty, and turned into clinics, so that some sufferers could be removed from their families. *Slainte* offers ingenious suggestions for isolating those who must stay at home: the construction of small sleeping huts in the garden, or of hanging balcony-rooms outside a window, or if that is impossible, of a tent against the window inside.

And the amazing thing about these makeshift methods is that they worked. Deaths from tuberculosis dropped by a thousand in the first two years of the Association's existence, and there were seven thousand fewer cases of the disease re-

ported. The medical world was startled and impressed. Lady
Aberdeen was elected President of the Royal Institute of Public
Health, and the first woman honorary member of the British
Medical Association. France gave her a *médaille d'honneur*, and
New York a prize. She had honour everywhere – except
among the Irish ruling class.

For most of these held that the Lord Lieutenant and his
lady should be decorative and hospitable figure-heads and
nothing more. They saw Lady Aberdeen's activity as a tacit
reproach to their own callousness and neglect, and so, of
course, it was. For the basic cause of Irish T.B. and infant mortality was poverty, as the Nationalist movement had been
pointing out for a considerable time; the Vicereine seemed positively to be allying herself with these revolutionaries. Her own
editorial comments in *Slainte* were guarded, but one might
read between the lines, and she allowed more outspoken ones
to appear in articles by parish priests, who knew all about the
slums, urban or rural, in which their flocks had to dwell.
None of this increased her popularity with the landowners, or
with upper-middle-class Dublin, already suspicious of a viceregal couple who were advocates of Home Rule.

Lady Aberdeen played into their hands to some extent, by
economizing on state entertaining as much as she could, in
order that every penny should be devoted to her welfare work.
She was here in error, and should have budgeted more for the
weaknesses of human nature, but it is hard not to feel sympathy
with her, and indignation at the legend, still current, that the
Aberdeens were unpopular, stingy and mean. To this day, you
may meet elderly people in Dublin who recall with disgust the
children's parties at the Viceregal Lodge: 'I was so looking
forward to it, and I got a plainer tea than I'd have had in the
nursery at home.'

The Aberdeens had come to Ireland wealthy, and when they
left they had almost bankrupted themselves, and had to sell
portions of the Haddo estate in order to settle with their
creditors. The Wimbornes, who succeeded them, were also
wealthy and spent only a fraction of their wealth, (admittedly
in a much shorter term of office) and they have left a gracious
memory of hospitality and charm. The moral is plain: if you

wish to go down in history as a benefactress, don't do the children's teas on the cheap.

Even Sir Horace Plunkett, sad to record, failed to appreciate Lady Aberdeen as he ought to have done. He and she had been comrades in arms during the first tenure of office, when he was forming his co-operative movement and she nurturing her home industries; but the success of the W N H A seems to have alarmed him and provoked a sort of jealousy, and he could be heard muttering about titled busybodies. Even in the most enlightened of Irishmen, the fear of petticoat government runs deep. But it is doubtful if he would have actually opposed her, and in any case his connection with the Department had ceased. George Fletcher continued to be her close ally, and to recognize his work and hers as complementary.

The real enemy was Sir Henry Robinson, secretary of the Irish Local Government Board, under whose jurisdiction (in default of an Irish Health Minister) the country's health came. Sir Henry had been thirty years in the department he now headed, and he was getting round to all the needful reforms, gradually, correctly, having first ascertained that there were adequate finances and properly trained personnel. He had no need of a whirlwind Vicereine, backed by a team of amateurs and dependent on charity, to teach him his business. True, by the time he got around to it all himself, so many thousands more young people would have coughed out their lives, and so many thousands more babies been stillborn, but that was just unfortunate. In short, his was the typical bureaucratic mind.

At first he tried flattery on Her Ex: 'It is perfectly marvellous – all this work about cleanliness, health and disease prevention. You really ought to be made into a Public Department . . .' coupled with warnings on the need to proceed with caution and consolidate one's finances. When he found himself by-passed, it was open war between them, and they were continually rushing to London to get Lloyd George's ear, or to glare at each other across a Treasury table. And when Lady Aberdeen finally secured a Government grant of £25,000 for the building of the much needed tuberculosis hospital in the Dublin hinterland, Sir Henry's fury knew no bounds. He actually wrote to the Treasury protesting against the money being handed over to 'an association of irresponsible women,' and Her Ex had to make another journey to Whitehall to prove that she had the backing of every County Council in Ireland, and that every step in her plans had been taken in consultation with them. She won, and Peamount Hospital is now her finest memorial in Ireland – or perhaps one should say, the hospital plus the fact that only a portion of it is now needed for tubercular cases, the rest being used as a home and workshops for mentally defective boys.

But the hostility of a Government department added to her difficulties, and though one can't suppose that an official of Sir Henry's standing spread adverse rumours about her work, still he did not go out of his way to contradict them. Constance felt the backwash; in some areas she found that people believed the W N H A was harming trade, or that those who took tuberculosis tests might lose their jobs, and she had to get the parish priest to set such fears at rest.

And when he came to write his memoirs, Sir Henry repeated with relish the legend that the caravan 'Eire' spread terror in the west, with its demonstration slides and cultures of bacilli, audiences objecting that 'some of them microbes might escape and be attacking quiet people at night, when it was too dark to see them and get out of their way.' Well, perhaps such an incident did occur in some remote spot, but he says nothing of the hundreds who walked over the hills to hear a new message of life and hope.

On Lady Aberdeen personally, Sir Henry is blandly regretful. 'More Irish than the Irish . . . a want of proportion . . . surrounded by advisers who gave way to her in everything, and never liked to risk offending her by warning her of financial danger . . . I was unfortunate enough to be one of those who had constant disputes with her, but they never blinded me to the fact of her meritorious efforts for public health reform, and I never ceased to regret that she was not better advised.'* We need not take any of this too seriously. Lady Aberdeen kept her finances steady by her fund-raising campaigns and her personal

* 'Memories Wise and Otherwise', by Sir Henry Robinson, KCB, Cassell, 1924.

sacrifices; she was not a woman to listen to flatterers, as he himself knew; and all that the last sentence reveals is his chagrin that she was not advised by him.

In the April, 1910, issue of *Slainte* Constance reports on a series of lectures she has been giving in factories – Armagh in January, Dundalk in February, in March Drogheda, and then Castlecomer in County Kilkenny. Her account of this last has about it an unusual glow. She stayed with the local big family, the Prior-Wandesfordes, and first gave a week of lectures in the little town; then a second week at the Colliery School attached to the anthracite mines which the family owned. The miners themselves came to her evening lectures and proved to be keen students. 'Their bandaging is excellent, and I am indebted to them for the first practical experience of a pit stretcher. They intend forming a First Aid Corps, and I should like to take this opportunity of wishing them every success, and also of expressing my thanks to those whose kindness and help made the fortnight a delightful one.'

She does not, naturally, tell the readers of *Slainte* that the engineer in charge of the mine had fallen violently in love with her, though it no doubt added to her agreeable feeling of success. It is most unlikely that she took him seriously at first; she made friends and admirers wherever she went. She continued with her round of lecturing, and was busier than ever that summer. But James Heppell Marr told a friend that he was fascinated by this young woman, who was so gay and wore large hats with an 'air'. He could not get her out of his mind.

Castlecomer is not an impossible distance from Dublin, and he began a dogged and persistent courtship. He was not in the least what the Fletchers had imagined or wanted for Constance. Etty would have liked her to marry a titled admirer whom she is known to have refused, and George probably hoped it would be one of the clever young men on his staff. But she was twenty-four, and old enough to know her own mind, and when, to their astonishment, she eventually accepted Marr, there was nothing more to be said.

They gave her a grand wedding, on 10 November 1910, at St Philip and St James in Booterstown, the church they had attended since Blackrock days.* Their Excellencies honoured her by signing the register as her principal witnesses. Gilbert, who was a page, remembers that Arnold and Donald bought a fake ink-spot from a joke shop, and placed it on the wedding gown just before she was due to dress. It was the sort of silliness guaranteed to make any bride jumpy, but Constance's outburst of hysterical fury was so unexpected, and so unlike her, that they were all shaken. It is allowable to guess that she saw more than her wedding dress in ruins, and that already she knew in her heart that she was making a terrible mistake.

* In her autobiographical notes, Constance charts the family progress from the less to the more fashionable religious denominations: Presbyterian in Derby, Methodist in Plymouth, Congregational in Moseley, in Dublin Church of Ireland.

2. CONSTANCE MARR

Why she did it remains a mystery. The obvious explanation –
to get away from home – will scarcely hold. She had had better
chances, and she gave up an exciting career as a leading member
of Lady Aberdeen's team, with Her Ex as a delightful substitute
mother. She must have genuinely believed that she was in love.

Heppell Marr was a widower, with a beautiful little girl by
his first marriage. He had a pleasant Irish Georgian stone house,
about a mile out of Castlecomer, at the hamlet of Coolbawn.
The house was desolate and the garden derelict, but both had
great possibilities, and Constance could picture herself making a
happy and gracious life for him and for Joan. And probably,
like many another lively clever girl, she was excited at having
aroused so much passion in a strong, silent man. She did not
appreciate that his taciturnity and dourness were the opposite
of her warm, expansive temperament, that they really had no
interests in common, and that unlike the miners and the schoolchildren, he never would become a member of her team.

Even so, the marriage might have worked if the physical side
of it had been a success. Constance, as a health lecturer, must
be supposed to have known the facts of life in theory, but an
Edwardian upbringing was rigidly compartmentalized, and
she knew little of them in practice; in practice she found she
did not care for them at all. And this came very hard on Marr,
the one who was really in love. He found himself rejected in
the way that is most humiliating to a man's pride. He had a
naturally quick temper, which easily became a violent one.
He would shout at her, and there may even have been physical
violence. Arnold, visiting them soon after the marriage, was

infuriated by the way he heard his sister spoken to, and when the two youngest boys came to stay they were scared of him, and they felt that Constance and his daughter Joan were scared of him too.

There are elements of a Soames-Irene situation, but Galsworthy is careful to put pressures on Irene which practically force her to marry Soames. Constance had been under no pressure to marry Marr; she had done it of her own free will. To her other troubles was added isolation. It was always essential to Constance to be one of a band, and preferably its leader. After her radiant first visit she had no doubt seen herself as a leader in Castlecomer, but it was a very different matter when she came to live there, with no other social position than that of the mine engineer's wife. The Prior-Wandesfordes had never seen much of Marr socially, regarding him as a rough diamond, but when he brought home the Vicereine's protegée, though they could not imagine how he had persuaded such a girl to marry him, they did their best to be kind. But their interests, and those of the neighbourhood, were mainly sporting, and Constance, except for an occasional racecourse flutter, cared nothing for sport.

She made a brave effort to build a life out of disaster. The possession of her own first house and garden was a very real pleasure, especially as both were susceptible of infinite improvement. She has described in *A Garden Notebook* this first garden, a tangle of weeds, and her 'poor delicate handyman, my only assistant. He carted water for the house, groomed a horse, carried in turf for fires, undertook dozens of chores, and, when he thought about it, did a little gardening.' Between them they pulled the garden round, built a pergola and dug stones from the stream-bed to make a path beneath it, and got rid of the weeds – and she, in her ignorance, pulled up a fine stand of Gladwyn Iris too. Having flowers to pick, and to grow specially for picking, increased that feeling for line and colour of which her father had observed the beginnings.

Within doors, there was no one to keep her out of the kitchen, and though, as an Irish country lady, she had servants, they were ignorant girls to whom everything must be taught. Shops were distant and inadequate, and the bread uneatable;

with a dough-mixing machine Constance made her own. Vera Prior-Wandesforde, the schoolgirl daughter of the Big House, remembers how impressed her parents were by young Mrs Marr's dashing housekeeping and experimental food. It found less favour with Marr's chief crony, the Prior-Wandesforde land-agent, another rough diamond. 'I can't stand those sort of kickshaws', he proclaimed, and the neighbourhood had a good laugh. It was the sort of story Constance delighted to tell against herself in later years, but it cannot have amused her at the time.

And then there was the care of her six-year-old stepdaughter. But Joan Marr has retained no cheerful memories of these years. There was no question of unkindness; it was not in Constance to be unkind to a child. But she could not give to this first little girl in her life the sense of creative excitement and confidence that she would later give to hundreds of others. She was too oppressed and dispirited herself.

Lacking a kindred spirit of flesh and blood, she made a friend for herself out of a book, which had been given to her, presumably as a wedding present; 'it became a sort of Bible to me,' she says. It was *Pot Pourri from a Surrey Garden*, by Mrs C. W. Earle, and though it is a completely (though unjustly) forgotten work today, it was to have a lasting effect on her own thought and writing, and can with advantage be re-opened here. The title suggests something discursive, which it is – gardening, cookery, general reflections, scraps of poetry, jumbled as they come from the writer's mind – and also something pretty-pretty, which it certainly is not. There are three hundred and fifty pages of close, unillustrated type, the product of a shrewd, disillusioned and wide-ranging mind.

Theresa Earle had blue blood and brains on both sides of her family; her father was a Villiers, her mother a Lidell. The father died young, and the mother brought her children up cheaply on the Continent; they were well-connected poor relations, and at a pinch there was always a home with our uncle the Ambassador or our cousin the Minister. Theresa was the eldest and had the mortification of seeing her sister Edith married before her, and to the very man who would have suited herself: Robert Lytton, later Earl of Lytton and Viceroy of India. Rather than remain on the shelf, at twenty-seven she married Captain Earle, where thereupon retired from the 6th Rifles, did nothing else for the rest of his life, and seems to have been both delicate and dull. She made the best of it, bore him three sons, and comments coolly in her autobiography (published, of course, long after his death) on 'my two vocations, to nurse my husband, and to be a good poor man's wife.'

She was a keen Liberal from the age of eighteen, and her greatest delight was to talk politics, preferably with her adored brother-in-law. At the height of his viceregal glory he still found time to write letters to his 'dearest Theresa'. Her circle in London included Watts, Burne-Jones, the Huxleys, and George Eliot who was 'specially friendly and nice to me.' And although badly off by the standards of her class, she had two houses, in London for the winter, in Surrey for the summer, where 'kitchen-garden, flower-garden, house and drive can scarcely cover more than two acres.'

Having no daughter, she was devoted to her Lytton nieces; it was to please them that she wrote *Pot Pourri*, and one of them, Constance, contributes an appendix on Japanese flower arrangement which has the book's sole illustration. Lady Constance Lytton: the name rings a bell, and then one realizes that this is the young woman who will later become a Suffragette heroine and martyr, her health permanently ruined by her treatment in prison.

Captain Earle, negative and timorous as ever, first urged his wife not to write a book, and then not to publish it. He received his presentation copy in 1898, and had time to read it and decide that after all it did not disgrace him, before mounting his bicycle and riding off to meet his death in a road accident.

His widow, at sixty, now had opening before her a far more congenial career. Today a Theresa Villiers would not need to marry a Captain Earle; she would probably become a Member of Parliament, and end up as a Life Peeress. But the extraordinary success of her books – *Pot Pourri* went into eighteen editions within a year, and its sequels were equally well received – must have come in part because she spoke to a generation of frustrated women, and showed them how to make the best of their lot. 'A spirit of benign and motherly materialism broods over the book,' wrote one critic of *Pot Pourri*, and the author finds this 'an expression I thought rather nice, as it was what I had aimed at.'

Gardening was her chief artistic outlet, and she followed the teachings of William Robinson, but not uncritically; she decided, for instance, that the 'wild garden' he so warmly advocated would need a lot more upkeep than tame ones. She was a contemporary of Gertrude Jekyll, and she praises *Wood and Garden*, but on a note of slight patronage; the author appears to her to be a sort of superior nurseryman. Some of her remarks on flower-arrangement have a Spry-like sound. There is an all-white dinner table, there is a flower table, 'which does flowers or plants much more justice than dotting them about the room', there is a plea to leave chrysanthemums undisbudded, 'bunches of chrysanthemums with their buds will go on blooming a long time in water, and make in a room a natural and beautiful decoration, instead of painfully reminding one of the correctness of the flower's paper imitations.' (For 'paper' read 'plastic' and the remark is just as applicable today.)

But as there are no illustrations, Mrs Earle's actual arrangements cannot be said to have influenced Constance's. They were probably, like Miss Jekyll's, better in theory than in practice.

In Constance's copy of *Pot Pourri*, the sections underlined or pencilled in the margin are not those on gardening, but those on education, and particularly the chapter 'Daughters'. For Mrs Earle expresses and elucidates what Constance had been obscurely feeling, that the academic education so prized by her father was not necessarily the right one for women like herself.

Mrs Earle is no reactionary. She is proud of her clever Lytton nieces; she holds that a girl with a real vocation for a career should be given the same facilities to train for it as a man. But she warns that the vote so ardently campaigned for will prove no short cut to feminine equality and prosperity, and that a degree will not lead automatically to a good job, and who is to say that she was wrong? She considers it almost impossible for a woman to keep on her profession after marriage; in fact, the professional woman earning any sort of reasonable salary in the 1890s was better off in the matter of staff than her counterpart today, dependent for the care of home and children on au-pair girls with a four months' average length of stay. That thousands of young married women do hold down full-time jobs under these conditions proves our sex to have more resilience than Mrs Earle budgeted for; but the cost in nervous tension must be prodigious.

In Theresa Earle's view, the great majority of women wish to marry – and again, who shall gainsay her? For all but those with a strong vocational bent, therefore, it is useless to plan a career as a man plans his; the lottery of marriage will bring them something quite different. Adaptability should be the principal aim of their training. 'The longer I live, the more I believe that a woman's education, if she has not to learn some special trade, should be awakening and yet superficial.' One winces at that last word, but she goes on to explain that she does not mean the dictionary synonym of 'shallow', but 'something which gives a desire in the child or the girl to learn. Instead of boring her to death with what teachers consider the roots and foundations of knowledge, I would strive to arouse curiosity, and trust that she would go deeper herself when the desire for knowledge came.'

In a further passage underlined by Constance, Mrs Earle stresses the value of their wandering childhood to herself and her sister: their governess education ceasing at the age of twelve, left with occasional masters to learn what they chose thereafter, never staying in one place for more than six months at a time. 'Many parents are so afraid of making these breaks in the continuity of their girls' education, and – as is only human – the governesses and teachers are always against it. One of the disadvantages of classes and competitive education is that ambitious children themselves often object to their studies being broken into. But all the experience of moving about, the little hardships and privations that come even in our modern luxurious travelling, are an immense advantage and training to children . . . The impressions gained through the eyes and ears are incomparably more lasting and real than any information learnt from books.' To Constance, with her hatred of 'competitive education', such words were balm, and if her own schooldays had not been quite so peripatetic as Mrs Earle's, still there had been disruptions enough.

And the whole tenor of Mrs Earle's argument – whether she is advising on gardening, or on entertaining, or on the prosecution of a hobby like her own of collecting old gardening books – is that a woman's lot (at any rate if she be an upper-class lady) can be a truly creative one. She may even suspect, though she is too much a Victorian to say so, that it can be more creative than the allegedly more important profession of the husband. Certainly her own was more creative than that of poor Captain Earle, who had passed half a lifetime in retirement from the 6th Rifles.

Education had always been the primary concern of the Fletcher family, but on the reasons for Constance's particular interest in these passages I can, of course, only speculate. She was carrying a child, who might have been born a daughter, and she may have been planning how that daughter should be brought up. But I think it more probable that already she was planning to escape from the dead-end into which her misjudgment had brought her, return to her true bent, and one day have a school, a new and different sort of school, of her own.

Lady Aberdeen continued to keep in touch with her favourite, and her Christmas present for 1911 was a beautiful little diary for 1912, with 'Constance' embossed in gold on its red morocco cover, and an inscription reading: 'Dedicated to the use of Constance Marr, in the hope that she may have much happiness and much blessing and much helpful service to record during 1912. I. A.' Constance was not much of a diarist, but her other diaries do at least show engagements. This one is empty.

Yet one important event did occur during the year; her son Anthony Heppell Marr, was born on March 23rd. Both the Aberdeens stood godparents, and the event brought happiness to the baby's father and grandfather. Essentially a man's man, Heppell Marr adored his baby son, and George Fletcher was equally devoted. Of Constance, it can be said that she was a good mother but not a besotted one, her maternal instinct tending to spread itself over large numbers of children. But she kept Tony with her through all her vicissitudes, struggled to give him the best possible education, and always had his interests at the back of her mind. If they were not always quite at the front of her mind, that was because so many others competed for the position.

His coming, however, did not improve relations between husband and wife. Constance had had a long and agonizing labour, and she seems to have determined that he should be an only child. A photograph of her taken a year later, with the baby on her knee, is the only one quite without trace of her characteristic vitality. She looks thin, defeated and despairing.

The outbreak of war in 1914 was for the Marrs an order of release. There was no conscription in Ireland, but Heppell Marr volunteered (as did Constance's elder brothers) and secured a commission. A natural soldier, he was a Captain in the Royal Irish Fusiliers by March of 1915.

Constance was swept back into Lady Aberdeen's orbit. Her Excellency had pounced upon the Department, and George Fletcher in a letter to her later on recalled 'how you pressed a somewhat unwilling Department into service, and how in spite of lions in the path you were the cause of our training nearly ten thousand VAD's.' A salaried post as lecturer for Constance was made in the Department itself, and to this she added the secretaryship of the Dublin Red Cross, which allotted her a small office in the Castle. She also resumed the health lecturing to mothers and schoolchildren. For Lady Aberdeen was still concerned at the high rate of infant mortality, and her *Slainte* editorials stress that there is more than ever need to save a country's babies in time of war.

Constance in *Slainte* reports on her child-welfare section at the big Civic Exhibition which she had helped Lady Aberdeen to organize; she particularly enjoyed the visits of the schoolchildren and their questions. 'The children were interested because they were hearing about things which belonged to their everyday lives, and learning of something they might actually carry out themselves, and that is joy to any healthy child.' Charts showed them the hours of sleep they ought to have at different ages, and gave warnings about fires and dangerous toys, and Constance comments that in poor families the care of younger children falls largely on the older, and therefore details of baby-bathing, dressing and feeding are of intense interest.

The senior Fletchers now lived out at Shankhill. Constance, with the two children and a nurse to look after them, had moved into a small flat near Leeson Street; flats were still a novelty in Dublin, and it is remembered how pretty and unusual she made hers. She cannot have had much time to enjoy it, with her arduous days and evenings of lecturing, fund-raising, planning concerts and subscription dances, and with responsibility for a night canteen at the National Shell Factory to crown all. But she is remembered as a wonderful organizer, always inspiring, elegant and gay. 'I think we all had a bit of a crush on her,' says Miss Eva Hackett, who trained under her as a young VAD. The remark is revealing, and can be echoed down the rest of Constance's life. She was no longer just a satellite of Her Ex. She had become, in her own right, the leader of a team.

In December of 1914, a blow fell upon the Aberdeens. Mr Asquith decided that a nine years' viceroyalty was long enough, and that he would replace them by the Wimbornes. Protests came in from all over Ireland, but his mind was made up (had Sir Henry Robinson, one wonders, influenced it?). They were given a marquisate as a very poor compensation, and left officially in February, but Lady Aberdeen was not one to abandon the principal interest of her life. She took a Dublin house as headquarters for the WNHA and as a pied-à-terre for herself, and set out with her husband on a two-year fund-collecting tour in America. While there, they heard the news of the Easter, 1916, Rising, and at least they were spared the anguish of being in official position at the time.

The Rising brought grimly practical experience to the Dublin Red Cross, and to Constance a St John silver medal for her organization of it. She ever afterwards remembered those violent weeks with horror, and would talk indignantly at the end of her life of having had to live 'through three wars'. To Gilbert and Lynton, still schoolboys, it seemed a lark. Against orders they came into Dublin to watch the fighting at the Leeson Street Bridge, and were lucky not to get bullets through their heads. George, as a Government official, was loyal to the Crown, but he had always been sympathetic to Irish national aspirations, and it says much for the high esteem in which he was held by men of widely differing political opinions, that he continued in office under the Free State, and retired at the natural term, with universal good wishes and praise. He is said to have been the last English official to quit Irish soil.

Dublin without Her Ex must have seemed a duller place to Constance. Her Red Cross work was now smoothly organized. and she had a good deputy to whom she could hand over; she may also have wished to get closer to the English war effort. These were not, I suspect, her main reasons for deciding to leave Ireland later in 1916. Heppell Marr's leaves had made a radical change in her family's attitude towards him. They had sided with her in her matrimonial troubles, but now he seemed to them a new man, and they began to appreciate his very real qualities. To Donald and Arnold he was a comrade in arms, to the younger boys a hero, and Etty, most unexpectedly, had taken to him a strong liking. ('Never liked your fiancé or your husband till you'd left them,' Constance drily records.)

A reconciliation, if only for the sake of the child, seemed to everyone desirable. Perhaps it even seemed so to Constance; Miss Hackett recalls that when she knew he was coming home on leave she would seem excited and pleased. But the actuality was as bad as ever. Her stepdaughter remembers the rows starting all over again, and now she was no longer prepared to be cowed and shouted at. She was financially independent, and could, in effect, walk out.

The great armaments firm of Vickers advertised a post as welfare supervisor to the women employees in their factories at Barrow-in-Furness. Constance applied, and with her excellent record and references, got it. She handed Joan back to her mother's family, tucked her little boy under her arm, and departed to England. And although she was to bear his name for six years more, it was the end of her marriage to James Heppell Marr.

‹‹‹‹‹‹‹‹‹‹‹‹‹‹‹‹

3. EAST END

The women munitions workers in Barrow came mainly from Ireland, and because recruitment had been hurried and expansion rapid, their living conditions were deplorable. Many were sleeping two and three to a bed. Constance in her short stay transformed the picture, with a whirlwind campaign for better lodgings, and with the establishment of rest rooms and canteens. The results she achieved commended her to inspectors from the Ministry of Munitions as the ideal choice for an important new job, as director of women's staff at the Ministry's aircraft production headquarters, the Hotel Cecil in London. She was accordingly released by Vickers in January of 1917, and came to London for the second time.

The heads of departments at the Ministry came from many walks of life; they were a cross-section of clever people, among whom she quickly made friends, and two of these were to have a lasting influence on her life. Marjorie Russell, known to everyone as 'John', had come from advertising to be the Ministry's public relations officer. She was exactly the contact a provincial newcomer needed, 'knowing everyone', and generous in sharing her wide acquaintance. She lived with a distinguished literary man, and as he was away on war service, she invited Constance and Tony to share her flat in St John's Wood. And Constance soon had need of a friend's support, for the Fletcher luck was running out.

In April, the family received news that Arnold was lying gravely wounded in the Red Cross Hospital at Rouen; his father went over, and found that among his nurses were some who had been trained by Constance in Ireland. Arnold died on

April 30th, and before George could return, there came another of the dreadful telegrams to Constance in London; Donald had also died of wounds, in Salonika, two days earlier. Gilbert, who was staying with her, made the long night journey back to Dublin, in order to break the news to his mother.

It shattered them all, and they were slow to recover. It horrified Dublin, too, for while such tragedies were common enough in England, Ireland, with no conscription, was not hardened to seeing the flower of a family wiped out. The story made the front page of the Dublin papers, and inspired a poem, *The Brothers*, by Katharine Tynan. She was a neighbour of the Fletchers at Shankill, had known both boys well, and the story of their hideout in the hills and their long tramps over the heather. In the poem she saw them inseparable still, 'unspent, footing the bracken.' It is among the best she ever wrote, and can compare in poignancy with the more famous elegy of Binyon.

Constance's work at the Aircraft Production Department was ably summarized by her immediate superior when he wrote her a letter of appreciation, as the Ministry of Munitions was being run down in 1919 and she herself was transferring to another job.

He reminded her (and her next employers) that she had been with the Department from its beginnings and had seen the number of women munitions workers grow to nearly three and a half thousand. She had had sole charge of their welfare, and been responsible for several thousands more in other parts of the kingdom.

She had organized medical treatment for them, under a woman doctor and a staff of nurses. She had secured and equipped rest and recreation rooms. She had got a sickness benefit scheme going, and had found and furnished a holiday cottage for those in need of rest or convalescence. She had helped plan training classes for the clerical staff, and it was on her advice that women staff officers had been appointed in all branches of the Ministry. She had made herself available to all members of the staff at all times, and her patience, sympathy and wisdom had smoothed over difficulties, righted injustices, and ensured a high standard of efficiency and morale. He deeply regretted that the Department was now to lose her, and assured her that she carried with her the good wishes of all her colleagues.

It was indeed a tribute, and from what we know of Constance and her gifts, no doubt a fully justified one. Nevertheless, it cannot be claimed that the writer was quite without *parti-pris*. The signature to the letter is that of H. E. Spry.

Constance, in her thirties, had found the man to suit her at last.

His Christian names were Henry Errnest, but to his older brothers he was the Little Shaver, or Shav, and this nickname stuck to him for life. He won scholarships to Merchant Taylors, and then to Sidney Sussex, Cambridge, but he was not physically strong, and the doctors recommended a career in a warm climate. Accordingly he joined the Indian Civil Service, and rose quickly on its legal and financial side. He was seconded, on the outbreak of war, to become Head of Personnel at the Aircraft Production Department, and thus the immediate chief of Constance Marr.

He was in most respects the antithesis of Heppell Marr: a man of the world, cultivated, witty, charming; a man, moreover, with a genuine liking for feminine company, and who experienced no difficulty in sharing feminine interests. He could enter into Constance's enthusiasms, her feeling for the beautiful things of life, for pictures and furniture and gardens and good food. His own instinct was to live *en grand seigneur* when funds allowed, but his financial ability and steady judgment would keep Constance on the rails. He was exactly what she needed, as lover, as comrade, as business associate. He was, as she said in one of her dedications, 'H.E.S. who makes all things possible.' She needed him desperately, and she acquired him. It was probably not very difficult. He had reached that stage in life when a man often seems to have more in common with the brilliant woman colleague than with the devoted wife at home.

For of course there was a wife, and there were two children of school age.

By April of 1919, when Constance left Aircraft Production for Inland Revenue, there to be deputy principal of women's staff, it must have been agreed between her and Spry that one day they would join their lives. The immediate prospects were not bright. Not only was it necessary for them to secure their respective divorces, but Spry, in order to be eligible for a pension, needed to put in two more years with the Indian Civil Service. He did not propose to stay longer than that, perceiving clearly that Indian independence was on the way. But when he returned, he would still be faced with the problem of making a new career for himself, in his late forties, and in the ruthless post-war world.

Spry left for India, and Constance set about getting her divorce. And here Heppell Marr behaved, as might have been predicted, with the utmost generosity. He took the technical guilt upon himself, so that her promising career in the Civil Service should not be interfered with. And this was now doubly important, because his own was in ruins. With a splendid war record and a D S O, he found himself, like thousands of other returned heroes, unwanted, and had to tramp the London streets looking for a job. Constance never denied him access to his son, but finally he was obliged to take another mining post in India, which effectively cut him off from the one thing that had mattered in his unhappy marriage. The little boy on his side never accepted Spry as a substitute father, always knew who his real father was, welcomed him with joy on his rare spells of leave, and wept when he went away again. But to the children of broken marriages, all this is a commonplace.

Constance did not remain long with the Inland Revenue. She was tired of being a civil servant, and longed to get back to her first interest, education. Indeed, studying the pattern of her life, it is easy to see that she invariably tired of anything that looked like becoming a rut. She was essentially an originator, an inspirer of enthusiasm in others. She would fling herself heart and soul into a new activity, get it on its feet, hand it over to people whose lives were permanently altered and enriched by their contact with her – and then move on herself to something else.

So when Sir Robert Blair offered her the headship of a new school in the East End, she accepted. Superficially, it could not have been more remote from the school for gracious living which she had envisaged as she turned the pages of Mrs Earle. But it embodied that intelligent woman's basic principle, that education should directly prepare for the sort of life the pupils are going to lead. And it was certainly quite unlike any other school that had been known in England before.

Few episodes in our social history have been braver or more generous than the passing of the 1918 Education Act. It was debated in the spring of that year, when the Germans were breaking through on the western front, and the nation seemed in greater peril than ever; it looked forward to a land fit for returning soldiers, and to a better deal for their children. All fees were to be abolished in state elementary schools, the leaving age was to be raised to fourteen, the salaries of teachers were increased. But the great novelty of the Act was the section which provided that all boys and girls between fourteen and eighteen who had not gone on to secondary or technical schools should compulsorily attend day continuation schools, their employers giving them leave from work, for one whole day or two half days per week.

Professor Dover Wilson, the Shakespearean scholar, was then an official at the Board of Education, and had been largely instrumental in forming the policy behind these new schools, and he explains it in some detail in his memoirs, *Milestones on the Dover Road*. The young wage-earner, having just left elementary school, would not want to go back to the same thing. He was eager for an adult life and outlook, and the curriculum of the continuation school should therefore be designed to help him take his place in the workshop, the factory or the office. But the training was not to be wholly technical: it should also open for him the doors of the theatre, the art gallery and the concert hall, and lead him to a fuller understanding of the adult world on whose threshold he stood.

It followed that elementary-school staffs were not ideal material for continuation-school teaching. They tended to be rigid disciplinarians, for which nobody could blame them; they had carried for sixty years the thankless burden of teaching the three Rs to huge classes in grim surroundings. Eventually, it was planned that the new schools should train their own staffs; in practice, there had to be initial recruitment from the elementary schools, if the scheme were to get started at all. But for the headships, the Board urged the local authorities, under whom the schools were to be run, to look for men and women with a knowledge of the world rather than of textbooks. In inviting the daughter of his old friend to head the Homerton and South Hackney Day Continuation School, Sir Robert Blair was not doing her a favour. He was appointing the right person for the job, and he must have wished that he had more like her.

A further problem was lack of buildings. There was no time to erect new ones; existing ones had to be found and converted, and the timetable was left to the local authorities. The 'compulsory' element in the Act was thus virtually negatived; it was robbed of its teeth. Dover Wilson and his colleagues viewed with dismay the lethargic attitudes of many authorities, reinforced by the pressures brought to bear on them by local employers; for Lloyd George's 'hard faced business men who had done well out of the war' hated the notion of continuation schools. Young labour was cheap labour, and if it had to be yielded up from shop or bench for a whole day every week, it ceased to be as cheap as all that. However, London under Blair's energetic direction set an example to the rest of the country. Constance and the other newly appointed heads started their own recruiting rounds.

She too must have wished she could persuade more friends to join her in a cultural crusade to the East End. She did persuade one, Josephine Cook, a sister of Marr's first wife, a beautiful and gifted woman who was to spend a good part of her life in the service of the Fletcher family. She was a qualified musician, and undertook the music and drama teaching of the new school; she also shared Constance's horticultural enthusiasm, and they moved out to a charming Jane-Austen cottage at Billericay, where Constance had the second garden of her adult life.

In luring away elementary school staffs, the new heads had an inbuilt advantage; they could offer secondary-school salaries. Florence Thurston, then a young teacher of sewing in a Stoke Newington school, remembers an inspector coming round to tell the staff of the new project and ask for volunteers, and how her headmistress gloomily remarked: 'the head of that queer new school is coming to pinch you.' And so it proved; the extra hundred pounds a year was welcome, but Miss Thurston found herself even more attracted by the fresh scope offered to her, and by the charm of Mrs Marr, though the actual working conditions were less salubrious than Stoke Newington, the genteel part of the area on which the Continuation School would draw.

The building allotted was in itself a dignified one, a Georgian mansion with portico and tree-lined drive, relic of the days when Homerton was a smart suburb and wealthy City merchants built their homes there. It stood at the corner of High Street and College Lane, and had been previously used as a teachers' training college. 'Amongst the tumbling and decaying Homerton houses, the school in comparison looked so stately and regal,' writes Lily Cullen, a pupil of those first years. Inside it was equally impressive, and 'your imagination was that you were miles away from the turmoil of traffic. You were suddenly brought back to reality by the smell of a pickle factory, and by glue smells, which penetrated the school.' It has all been swept away now, and a block of flats stands on the site.

Furniture, like everything else in those post-war years, was in short supply. The London County Council did their best, but at first the desks had no holes for inkwells, and the ink spilled everywhere. Constance would make continual forays to County Hall, often taking Miss Thurston with her. If she got no satisfaction from the supply department, she would breeze into Blair's room and perch on his desk. The great man hardly seemed to know how to defend himself against this familiarity, and she usually got what she wanted.

Somehow or other, the school started work in 1921, with an official opening a few weeks later by Mrs H. A. L. Fisher, wife of the President of the Board of Trade. Josephine Cook had assembled and rehearsed a choir, and a programme of school songs greeted the lady, who gave offence, no doubt unwittingly, in the staff room afterwards by observing that the public-school ethos of 'Forty Years On' could mean little to children from the slums. Constance replied gently that they did not see why stirring words and a fine tune should be the exclusive property of Harrow.

Everything was tentative and tricky. The mixed staff had to

accustom itself to working under a woman Head, (not that Constance, then or at any other time, found difficulty in getting men to work contentedly under her,) and to continually changing faces in the classrooms, as children came and went on their one or two days of schooling. The East End was still a tough place, and many of them were ragged and dirty; some were hungry. Employers to a man detested the scheme, threatened they would employ no child attending the school, or tried to keep young people back from attendance; and one of Constance's more alarming duties was to go round the shops and factories and make it clear she would have the law enforced. Sadly but understandably, a good many parents were also in opposition, and although it terrified her, she penetrated into slum homes and confronted enraged fathers. No one actually hit her when it came to the point; she must have looked too fragile and small.

And in appealing to parental pride, she seldom encountered a really hard heart. Some had actually encouraged their children to rowdyism and turbulence, in the hope that this would finish the school; she issued an open invitation to them all to come one evening and hear her point of view, and to a surprisingly large gathering, explained the practical advantages their children would gain from what the school had to offer. They listened, asked aggressive but sensible questions, and got spirited replies. Gradually the feeling of the meeting swung round to her. 'Now we'll have a concert,' she said. 'You all know *Old Folks at Home?*' Josephine Cook struck up on the piano, and in a trice she had the East End singing. It turned into a party. Henceforward, they were on her side.

No punishments or sanctions could be imposed in the continuation schools. The young people were obliged by law to come, but they had to be charmed to work. Some came rebellious, others prepared to lark about, but all who were pupils under Mrs Marr concur in remembering that the work was made so interesting that they wanted to do it. After the Victorian strictness of their previous schooling, they were being treated like adults, made to feel, as Lily Cullen puts it, 'alive and free'. Sinners were hauled before the Headmistress, and some went like roaring lions into her study; they came out smiling lambs. Nobody quite knows how she did it – except that whatever your crime, she always found something to praise in you first. 'We all have our blind spots and I suppose this is one of yours, but look how good you are at – ' carpentry, or book-keeping, or whatever it might be. The sense of failure and injustice under which many of them had been labouring melted away. The same miracle has been worked in our, very similar, post-war period by the best of the teachers in secondary-modern schools.

It is also agreed that she never made favourites, but naturally those children whose parents could afford to let them come two or three days a week – mostly those from the better-off Stoke Newington area – came most frequently under her eye, and some of them were promoted by her to be, in effect, prefects. One of these was Melora Cumings, who attended school three days a week, her subjects being French, English, History, Mathematics, Orthography and 'Practical'. She was summoned before the Head for having been impertinent, and it transpired that she had flared up in defence of backward 'truancy boys' at whom the teacher seemed to be sneering. Constance explained that she must not take the law into her own hands; the mistress was spoken to and decided her vocation lay elsewhere. The 'truancy boys' came from a special punitive school for consistent truants, this not being recognized then for what it almost invariably is, the symptom of an unhappy home. The boys were treated as unmanageable and potentially criminal, were humiliated by having to wear a uniform of short knickers, and were not supposed to mix with the rest. Constance would not have it. She drew the best out of them, and was justifiably proud that most of them made good.

There were other staff failures. The teacher in charge of an overflow class at a near-by chapel could not keep order, and her charges roamed at will through the passages or preached each other sermons from the pulpit; Constance would be obliged to round them up. But by the summer, she had gathered a team who understood what she was getting at and how to bring it about; and Miss Hunter, shorthand-typing, Miss Byrne, English-and-French, Mr Phipps, Book-keeping and Business Economics, Mr Jackson, Mathematics, Miss Cook, Music and Drama, are affectionately remembered in Hackney and Homerton to this day.

It was not in Constance's power to alter the curriculum, which was fixed by the LCC, but she did everything possible to humanize it and relate it to daily life. She could not hold classes in speech, manners and deportment, but she knew their importance to young people from poor homes, and Josephine Cook's two drama societies offered a valuable training which everyone was encouraged to take. Evening classes, for which there was soon a demand, were preceded by a little dance, with Miss Cook playing the piano; and once a month there was a full social evening attended by the staff. Sometimes these were in fancy-dress; Constance, it is remembered, came as a nun.

The boys' carpentry was encouraged to make attractive objects for the home, the girls' dressmaking to keep abreast of the styles. Materials were supplied by the LCC, and were limited in colour and design. Constance suggested to Miss Thurston that they should each make themselves a dress from the same pattern, in the same standard bright green, but with differently embroidered yokes. Miss Thurston worked a daisy-chain round hers; Constance's was solid with brilliant small flowers. When they appeared in their twin models, the effect on morale was electric. And Constance must have liked her dress, for she was photographed wearing it. On 'open days' dresses made by the class would be displayed on stands, something never before done in an LCC school.

Discussions of politics and current affairs were encouraged, and mock elections held; Conservative, Labour and Communist candidates were put up, and the Communist got in. The confidence to speak in public gained in this way would be an asset to many in the battles for better conditions that lay ahead.

But above all, Constance tried to satisfy the hunger for beauty that was apparent in these children who saw so little of it. She has described how a girl was brought before her for stealing ten shillings, which had not been spent on sweets but on paper flowers: 'I only wanted something pretty', wailed the culprit, and spoke straight to Constance's heart. She confessed to Melora Cumings that the grimness of the East End had at first come as a shock to her, 'but she had had to settle her mind to it, and so must we.'

The School must be an oasis of elegance. She herself was always beautifully dressed. 'The memory that is still vivid in my mind,' writes Lily Cullen, 'is of Mrs Marr sweeping into the school full of zest and flamboyance, always dressed very very smart and modern, which to us being young was a thrill, especially after our ordinary LCC teachers who were very Victorian and dowdy. Mrs Marr and our gym mistress, Miss Vine, believed in freedom of movement and expression, therefore we were taught not to wear corsets and suchlike. I have always been a rebel with regard to clothes and was one of the first to wear only a suspender-belt or roll-on, which I still wear (not the same one!).'

The school was painted in light colours, and Constance brought up flowers to decorate it from the cottage garden, where she and Josephine worked hard on Saturdays and Sundays, the only free time they had. Sir Robert Blair drew the line at supplying vases, so she set the children to colour-washing earthenware crocks, a technique she was later to use in her shop.

She made it a point of honour to keep the crocks filled with flowers, which she brought up in a basket from the Billericay garden. Her journey to school was long and complicated, and at first she hated it, but soon found that the flowers made her friends all along the route. The bus conductor, the ticket collector and her fellow passengers would all beg a buttonhole; even street urchins stopped her and asked for a flower, not a penny. Nothing could have brought home to her more clearly the hunger for flowers and natural beauty in the grimy streets of this, one of the dreariest parts of London.

She hardly ever reached the school with the contents of her basket intact, but enough must have remained to make a brave show, for the girls remember the privilege of being allowed to arrange them. No one claims to have been the first flower-arrangement pupil of the great Mrs Spry, and indeed few of them were aware that later on, Mrs Marr became Mrs Spry; but they admit that after they had done their best, she would sometimes add a small touch which made a mysteriously large amount of difference.

Tony, whose prep-school holidays were longer than those of Homerton, was allowed to spend the first and last days of term at the school, being given the run of the carpentry and handicraft rooms and treated as a general pet. There was competition to knit grey socks for his school uniform. And inevitably, there was speculation about Mrs Marr's private life, but it was generally assumed that like so many others, she was a war widow. Miss Thurston was sometimes entrusted with the posting of a letter to India; delicacy forbade her to look at the address. But she noticed that though Mrs Marr was always vivacious with the children and the staff, when she thought herself alone her face would often look anxious and sad.

However, a practical possibility of life together was opening out before herself and H. E. Spry.

His last two years in India had been spent as financial adviser to the Government of Bengal, and thus he came to the notice of the senior partner in a leading London firm of chartered accountants. He was offered a post as manager, with the promise of a partnership 'on the very day you qualify'. With considerable courage he accepted, and applied himself to the mastering of a new profession in middle-age – which, however, came easily to one with his innate financial abilities. His pay and Constance's salary meant that they could set up house in a modest but reasonable style. The cottage was too small for a household of four, so with Josephine Cook they moved into a small farmhouse at South Ockendon. The divorce was managed with the utmost discretion, and to the school and the LCC she continued to be known as Mrs Marr.

But to the Fletchers, the change in her status was another blow. Her divorcing Marr, whom they still regarded as their son-in-law, was bad enough; that she should replace him by a married man who had seen no war service seemed to them an aggravation, though the family bond was too close to be broken. They had to accept that she must do as she thought fit.

Over Heppell Marr, Constance might well feel that she had not much cause for self-reproach; her conduct towards the first Mrs Spry is another matter. Claire Spry is said to have received as a complete shock the news that she had lost her husband's affections even before his departure for India. Constance's life bears witness to her general kindness of heart, but there was also a ruthless streak, as no doubt there always is in people who make a mark in the world. *Take what you want and pay for it* . . . it seems to me that she paid.

From now on, it is possible to trace a change in her character. Alongside her happiness and fulfilment, there is a deepening of nervous fears, some of them quite irrational. It was as is she dreaded retribution, and not just the obvious one, that another woman might supplant her in her turn.

She who had travelled the length and breadth of Ireland came to hate travel, and had always to force herself to do it, feeling ill in trains and ships, flinching in cars to the distraction of the unfortunate driver, and absolutely refusing to set foot in aeroplanes. She who had worked closely with doctors was now so terrified of illness that she would never willingly consult one, nor, if she could help it, come into contact with anyone seriously ill. She who had spoken from platforms since she was twenty came to find every platform appearance an ordeal, to which she went twittering with nerves – though, as with most first-rate performers, the nerves disappeared as soon as she opened her mouth. She had never cared for solitude, but now she could not endure it for an instant; it was more than ever necessary to head a team.

The glorious flower arrangements, the serenely happy books, the vivacity and gaiety she presented to the world were all genuine; she was a person with an immense capacity for relishing life, and it was her gift to pass this on. But a darker current flowed beneath it; she was also a woman who never knew complete peace of mind.

And who is to measure the ingredients that go into a creative talent? Cosiness and comfort are rarely among them. Unalloyed happiness might have caused Constance to dwindle into a nonentity; the sense of insecurity was there to keep her alive and quivering, and needle her into work.

Although they were extremely poor until he qualified, both Spry and Constance had large ideas. The South Ockendon farmhouse was soon found too small and too suburban. The

8. With one of her favourite indoor plants – the Datura.

9. At work on the 'Christmas nonsense'. The mirror panelling behind her originally formed part of Norman Wilkinson's décor for Atkinsons' scent shop.

Old Rectory at Abinger, in one of the most charming 'mountain' parts of Surrey and with a rambling wild garden, was to let cheaply because it was not in a good state of repair. Despite this, and the long journey it involved for both of them, they moved in joyously on Boxing Day of 1926, and now had scope for the collecting of antiques and junk-shop finds which was a passion with them, and for the lavish ordering of a garden.

And here, good fortune sent Constance Walter Trower, who was to be her gardener for the rest of her life. He was a local boy, engaged to the girl who was doing parlourmaid duty in the house, and he needed a job, but he was doubtful of knowing enough about gardening to please Mrs Spry. She reassured him; she would teach him, she said, and so she did, but it was always a two-way traffic. And not always a completely harmonious one, for as Walter's skill and knowledge grew, his notion of what was due to the garden did not always square with her depredations for house and shop. But for her knowledge of plants he had a deep respect.

'I don't think anybody knew how poor she was in those days,' Walter says. 'But if there was a plant or bulb she wanted, she'd go without things for herself or for the house.' The first parrot and lily-flowered tulips to come on to the market after the war went into that garden – just one or two, all she could afford. But nothing Constance put into a garden was wasted. When she moved, the whole garden moved too, as Walter had good cause to learn.

In summer, a clothes-basket of flowers went up to London on the carrier of the car every morning, but now they were not only for the decoration of the school. News of her remarkable way with flowers had been spread abroad by Marjorie Russell and other former colleagues at the Ministry of Munitions, and she was often asked to do them for a dinner-table or a party; the commissions amused her, and the token payments were a welcome extra towards the garden's upkeep.

Her first regular customer, so he believes, was the cinema owner Sidney L. Bernstein, then a bachelor with a house in Albemarle Street. He had been employing a West End florist, but was never happy with the result. Marjorie Russell took him down to lunch at Abinger, and he fell in love, not only with

Constance's flowers but with her house and her whole way of doing things; here, he realized, was a sort of beauty that mere money could not buy. It was the touch of the inspired amateur, and he persuaded her to apply it in Albemarle Street every week.

In her turn she was his guest at a lunch party, where she met the stage designer Norman Wilkinson, who was equally enchanted with her flowers and with herself; it was a meeting of true minds. He told her that he was designing a shop for the perfumery firm of Atkinsons, on a site in Old Bond Street, that it would be quite unlike any shop that had ever been, that he wanted flowers in its windows which would be equally unlike florists' flowers, that she was the person to arrange them, and that she must turn professional and take a shop of her own. Their host, amused and interested, promised her that if she did, he would give her the bread-and-butter commission of supplying pot plants for the foyers of his chain of cinemas.

She was, she says, excited but terrified, and put off doing anything about it for a year. But it was a fact that she had been at Homerton as long as she ever stayed anywhere, that the school was running admirably and could be handed over to a successor, and that her husband was about to qualify as a chartered accountant, which would greatly improve their financial situation. If she were to make a change, the moment had come. In the summer of 1928 she handed in her resignation.

It was yet another disappointment for George Fletcher, whose pride in her achievement at Homerton had been great and justified. His friends were loud in their disapproval of someone who could give up a fine career in education for a silly little job like doing the flowers. It could not, at that stage, have seemed possible to anyone that doing the flowers would turn out to be a form of education too.

She was now moving into the world of wealth, luxury and fashion, and leaving behind her slums, dirt, poverty, malnutrition, all the demons against which Lady Aberdeen had trained her to fight. And if anyone had thought fit to reproach her on that score also, she could have replied with perfect truth that she had done her stint.

4. A BACK STREET FLORIST

During the year that she was summoning up courage to start a new career, Constance's friendship with Norman Wilkinson ripened, and was of immense benefit to her. He was the first artist she had known intimately, and just the sort of artist she needed to know – essentially a decorator, like herself. His exquisite little house on Chiswick Mall, so close to the Thames that at high tide there were often swans and mallards standing by the front door, was filled with beautiful furniture and bric-à-brac, the sort of clutter Constance loved to draw around her, and which he had been collecting much longer, and with much bigger resources, than she. One room contained old musical instruments, virginals, harpsichord, clavichord, which he not merely loved but played, for he was musically gifted too. In the tiny greenhouse he grew camellias, and in the tiny garden old roses, stocks, laced pinks, the sort of thing that could never be found in florists' shops.

He arranged them with originality and a delicate colour sense. On Constance's first visit, she found spring flowers in formal rectangles on the windowsills, and the pattern dragged at her subconscious mind. It was the picture of Richard the Second which she had admired so long ago in her father's copy of *The Studio*; and then she made a delightful discovery. It was Wilkinson as a young artist – he was only six years older than herself – who had painted it.

Norman Wilkinson was the younger son of a wealthy Birmingham family who owned 'a sort of Selfridges'. He is not to be confused, but of course constantly was, with his name-sake the distinguished marine painter, and at one period he signed himself 'Norman Wilkinson of Four Oaks' to emphasize the difference. The family early discovered they had a genius on their hands, put no pressure on him to join the business, and made his path as an art student easy – too easy, perhaps, for he always retained elements of the dilettante. He persuaded them to have William Lethaby design them a magnificent house in the Morris style, himself laid out the gardens, and found exactly the head gardener who could interpret his ideas. In the evenings, as the light failed, he would sit at the harpsichord in his parents' beautiful music room, quietly playing Bach. It was the perfect setting for his slender Roman elegance, and thus his friend the painter Keith Henderson remembers him still.

As students they had shared a studio in the Quartier Latin, where Wilkinson threw himself into all the artistic experiences Paris could offer, particularly the theatre and the opera. 'He had a connoisseur's flair for anything created by man with love,' Mr Henderson writes, 'whether pictures, sculpture, pottery, furniture, textiles, a flair that was really the result of a retentive memory for the minute differences between one piece and another. Flowers he adored. Stopping at a flower kiosk on the Boul' Mich' he would buy enormous quantities, to the flower woman's delight. I can see him in the studio, touching the flowers gently, as though they were human. His sensitive hands, strong yet blunt-tipped, would "feel" an object, like an octopus.' The same thing was often said of Constance's hands; it was as though she had an eye in the tip of each finger.

When Wilkinson returned to London from Paris, he gravitated naturally to stage design. He got to know Galsworthy, and through Galsworthy Granville Barker, for whom he did many decors in the famous Court Theatre seasons. Then the Shakespeare Memorial Theatre at Stratford on Avon claimed back this brilliant son of neighbouring Birmingham. He was its principal designer for several years, and his lovely *Twelfth Night* and all-silver *Midsummer Night's Dream* set a new standard. He was eventually made a Governor of the theatre.

With his friend Lovat Fraser, he did much to sweep away Edwardian stuffiness and bring a very English re-interpretation of Continental ideas to our stage. It is sadly ironic that owing to the ephemeral nature of their medium, and the relative shortness of their lives, both of them should now be so nearly forgotten. A few pottery figurines from Lovat Fraser's epoch-making *Beggar's Opera* at the Lyric, Hammersmith, linger no doubt on elderly mantelpieces. And Wilkinson has disappeared without trace, except for the glowing tributes paid to him in her books by Constance Spry.

Having a comfortable private income, he only took on work that amused him. He had never designed a shop before; nor, after Atkinsons, did he ever do one again. But the notion of a scent-shop took his fancy. It should be possible, he felt, to get away equally from the fake Pompadour or the dolled-up chemist's, which had been the ritual styles for such establishments (and for that matter still are). The shop was to be a fairy-tale setting of glass, specially made mirror glass, with a grey antique finish giving only blurred reflections, for walls and panelling, and with crystal chandeliers and a delicate fountain.

The site, one of the best in London, where Bond Street widens to receive Burlington Gardens, gave one large crescent-shaped window on the Bond Street frontage and three windows on the other. Wilkinson wished flower arrangements to hold the chief place in all four, and they must be the nearest that could be got to the flowers of the old herbals, scented if possible; above all nothing wired, no 'shop' flowers, nothing the ordinary florist would do. They must be flowers as done by a lady, but a lady of quite uncommon gifts.

'His designs for that exquisitely tranquil yet astonishing shop in Bond Street,' Keith Henderson writes, 'naturally impelled him to be eagerly on the lookout for someone of equal originality, who should be responsible for bringing them even more vividly to life with flowers. He found her. He told me about her. Her name was Constance.'

Constance's plan for her own little shop was modest in the extreme, compared to the lordly preparations at Atkinsons'. The account-books of her first, amateurish venture have not survived, so that it is impossible to say what capital she had, but it must have been tiny; probably a loan from Spry, the husband who 'makes all things possible', and who can have had small hope of ever seeing it repaid. A ground-floor shop with basement was rented at 7 Belgrave Road, a high-sounding address, but in fact leading from Victoria Station into Pimlico, and nowhere near the fashionable Belgrave Square. The shop had two small rooms at the back of it for offices, and the base-ment would make the work-room.

An early occupant was Florence Standfast, Constance's old acquaintance of the student hostel days, whom she encountered by chance in the Belgrave Road. Flo Standfast was working for an antique dealer, restoring and painting furniture; he paid her almost nothing and she was half starved. 'We can't have this,' Constance said, 'you must come and make artificial flowers for me.' Thus the important department ever afterwards known as 'the arts' was born out of the wish to help an old friend.

Her brother Gilbert and his Irish wife Marjorie, home on leave from colonial administration, helped her to get the shop ready. A paintbrush was put into Gilbert's hand, and he was told to stipple. He pointed out that he had no idea how to create this then novel effect. 'Nonsense,' said Constance, 'anyone can stipple.' Gilbert knew better than to argue with his sister; he stippled. When he returned to Africa, Marjorie stayed behind and joined the Abinger household, to help get the little concern on its feet.

The shop was christened Flower Decorations, the term Constance had invented to distinguish the work she did from ordinary floristry. But a florist was also engaged. It is customary to think of Constance as the woman who set flowers free from floristry, but in fact she had the highest regard for its speed and skill, which can only be acquired by years of apprentice-ship. What she deplored was the unnatural and ugly use to which this skill was so often put. A florist was essential for the wedding and funeral work which make up a large part of any flower shop's trade. As she herself remarks rather tartly: 'the sentimental young thing who wants only natural flowers at her wedding is likely to be disappointed by the result.'

Friends were pressed into service. The devoted Josephine Cook, still teaching music three days a week at Homerton, gave the rest of her time to the shop. Mr Phippen, the Homerton instructor in book-keeping, did its accounts. Marjorie Fletcher was the first saleswoman. But of course the main work devolved on Constance, who in that first year did the marketing and the flower decoration single-handed. She and Marjorie got up at 5.30 each morning in order to reach Covent Garden before the best stuff went. Homerton had been arduous enough; now, in her forties, she had taken on something tougher still. Yet this was the year in which she made her name, the year in which she may be said to have invented a new art.

Doing the great vases at Atkinsons for the first time was an occasion of mingled excitement and panic. The vases themselves had been provided by Wilkinson out of his junkshop finds, and she was introduced to the type of container she was afterwards to hunt so assiduously herself, and to popularize: soapstone and majolica urns, marble tazzas, carved wooden angels holding aloft cornucopias. They were in themselves an inspiration, but the season of the year was not, it being November, when Covent Garden could furnish little except chrysanthemums, or the Chinese lanterns and dyed statice which were all that 'drieds' amounted to at that time. To rely on such shopworn material would produce the very effect of *déjà-vu* against which Wilkinson had inveighed. But what was the alternative?

Then an Abinger neighbour came in from a walk with an armful of autumn leaves and berries, old man's beard, and golden trails of hops. The thought of all this soft, glowing colour in the soapstone urns kindled Constance's imagination, but would the authorities at Atkinsons feel they had been fobbed off with mere weeds? She took the basketful up with her to Covent Garden, and there saw some stems of rich green orchid which would make a weighty centrepiece for the light and flowing autumn glory. The result was as original as it was beautiful, and Wilkinson was enchanted.

From this experience she learnt two reassuring lessons: that wild material from the hedgerows and sophisticated material from the greenhouse could happily combine, and that there was no season so unpropitious that it could not produce treasures for those who had eyes to see. After that, she scrutinised everything before allowing Walter Trower to cart it away to his bonfire. 'From then on,' she says, 'the lamentations of passing summer and the sadness of autumn lost their sting; there was still so much to discover and to use.'

Wilkinson did not lose interest in his creation. All through the first year he watched and guided her. When things were right there was warm praise, constructive criticism when they fell short, and always enthusiasm and encouragement. And encouragement, from one who was himself an acclaimed artist, was what she most needed. It restored her self-confidence, and wiped out that long-ago, but never forgotten, shame over failing her father in the matter of the drawing lessons. 'You can have no idea, unless it has happened to you too,' she writes, 'how wonderful it is to come out of the dark frustration of being unable to crystallize such visions as you may have, and to find suddenly a possible medium of expression.'*

He had also given her a window on the world. No one going up or down Bond Street could possibly miss Atkinsons, and the flower arrangements were spotlit at night. The soapstone urns and the black marble tazza (or perhaps the carved wooden angels with a piece in alabaster or majolica) stood as if on the stage of a theatre. After all, Wilkinson was primarily a theatre man.

And people did notice, did stop and stare. Those great groups, majestic yet ethereal, were totally unlike anything that had been seen before, different in colouring, in blending of materials, above all in line. That marvellous downward swoop and droop – how in the world was it done? How were the laws of gravity defied, to have great trails and branches coming out of a shallow vessel on a long stem and sweeping the ground? How did the stems remain under water? Why didn't they die? The means of support – in those days just crumpled chicken wire, for the Japanese weighted lead pinholder had not yet reached London and the 'moisture-retaining substance' was yet further off – were so cunningly camouflaged that one could see nothing, though one pressed one's nose against the pane.

It was some two years later that I, as a young journalist starting on my first job in London, saw the windows at

---

* *Favourite Flowers,* p. 28.

Atkinsons, and like so many others I stopped in my tracks, utterly bemused. I had 'done the flowers' at home, and loved gardening, for years, yet suddenly realized that I knew nothing. It was autumn again, and in the black marble tazza there were the grey lichened branches that were one of Constance's most startling introductions, and strange frilly leaves, some grey, some purple, which I quite failed to recognize as kale, some crimson and purple flowers, dahlias perhaps, or roses, some scarlet toadstools ... a bunch of purple grapes ... Val Pirie denies that there were ever toadstools, and no doubt she is right, they were probably the scarlet spikes of wild-arum berries. Anyway, all Autumn was there, lavish and overspilling, like the Keats ode. 'Like a painting', people said, but I never felt that about the constantly changing pageant of the windows. Sculpture would be a nearer equivalent, for it is three-dimensional, but they were not sculpture either. They existed in their own right; genuinely, a new art.

Is distance lending enchantment? Possibly, for it is a drawback of all the applied arts, that they do rely to some extent, for their impact, upon novelty and surprise. I never remember seeing a piece that was a failure, but looking through the illustrations to her first book, *Flower Decorations,* (published in 1934, but work on the illustrations would be considerably earlier,) I am bound to concede that some of the groups look stiff and amateurish by today's standards. Constance, like most artists, improved as she went on. But in this book there are already a good many compositions, 'Green Table Decoration' for instance, or 'Shell of Nasturtiums', or 'Wall Vase with Mixed Bunch', or 'Mixed Bunch in Alabaster on Black Stand', which are as beautiful as anything she ever did. The two Mixed Bunches epitomize, for me at any rate, what came to be called the Spry Style.

Constance had novelty on her side, and Wilkinson to say '*étonne-moi*' as Diaghileff did to Cocteau; he was never content to let her do this week what she had done last. (She was later to apply the same goad to her own pupils.) But there is more to it than that. The person who discovers a virgin field in any art, and has first run in it, achieves an effect of spontaneity and excitement which can never quite be recaptured, even though successors may have equal vision and greater technical ability. Constance could astonish us in the nineteen-thirties because she too was a discoverer. She was perpetually astonishing herself.

So frequently did Constance express her indebtedness to Norman Wilkinson that some might conclude he taught her her art. This, of course, was not so. He gave her a splendid opening, and he was critic, guide and friend, but she was already doing flower work of originality when he met her. How did she evolve it?

The obvious answer is, from her girlhood familiarity with the work of the Dutch and Flemish flower painters. She is in the European tradition, based on an idealization of the bunch held in the hand, not in the Oriental, based on an idealization of the growing plant. But here too, her indebtedness needs qualification.

For one thing, not all the arrangements in Dutch pictures are of equal value; some are so stodgy that one suspects Mijnheer or Mevrouw must have insisted on doing them themselves, in order to ensure proper prominence for the striped tulip which had cost them a fortune. Then, in the earlier pictures, there are symbolic and religious significances which would mean nothing to Constance. And an examination of the great flower canvases will show that many of them could never actually have 'worked'. The flowers of spring and summer are out together, gravity is defied, branches and tendrils are poised without means of support. The individual items have been minutely studied from Nature, but the two-dimensional 'arrangement' has been made in the artist's mind.

The Dutch and Flemish painters gave her an idealized series of what one might call dream vases; she had to work out for herself how to make them come true. Her favourites were the painters of the two centuries between 1550 and 1750, particularly Jan Davidsz, Cornelius de Heem, Abraham Mignon, Jan van Huysum, Jan Breughel the elder. What she took from them was their feeling for mass and line, their opulence, the loving care with which they brought out the individual personality of leaf or flower, their contrasts of texture – contrasts which she also used to great effect in her gardening. When the young learner-decorators in the shop had time on their hands, she would send them round to the Medici Gallery to buy postcard reproductions of the classic flower pieces, and these were pinned up on the workroom wall or carried round in handbags, till their lessons sank in.

It is significant that she found the postcards perfectly adequate. She was not really interested in painting as such; she took what she wanted for her own art, and for her purpose a cheap reproduction would do just as well. She was no more than an average frequenter of museums and galleries; indeed, she had not the time. She never bought an original flower painting, though she did, as soon as she had the money, make an important collection of eighteenth and early nineteenth-century flower books; these, along with her vases and bric-à brac, were the tools of her workshop. Occasionally she would reproduce as a group a later French still-life, such as Fantin-Latour's artless basket of roses, but generally speaking, attempts to translate one art in terms of another seemed to her best left alone.

The other debt she acknowledged was not so much to Mrs Earle, whose 'charming ideas' existed only in the form of print, as to Gertrude Jekyll. 'I do respect and value her writing and her guidance,' she says in *Favourite Flowers*, and her copy of Miss Jekyll's *Flower Decoration in the House*, (published 1907), has the worn look of a volume much consulted.

In knowledge both of gardening and of painting – she had been trained as a painter, and only took up garden design when her sight weakened – Gertrude Jekyll was far ahead of Constance Spry. Her ideas, always sensible and often brilliant, are imparted with a governess-like severity which is in marked contrast to Mrs Earle's worldly charm. With Miss Jekyll we are gardening, not so much to amuse ourselves or to create beauty as to improve our moral characters. She is not quite so stern in the matter of flower arranging, but at the end of Chapter I we are reminded that it is no good 'shirking' the trouble of providing holders of suitable form. The use of words like 'shirk' make Miss Jekyll, for all her gifts, an unattractive writer to a generation which is no longer willing to be scolded into harmony and plenty like the tenants of Lady

Catherine de Bourgh; and I doubt if she will ever again be much read, though her influence will always be felt on our gardens by remote control.

The text of her flower-arranging manual is full of hints that Constance obviously pounced upon: the use of pale colours to complement each other instead of garish contrast; the massing rather than dotting of colour; the use of foliage, by itself or as a background to flowers, and of fruit with autumn flowers; the desirability of one handsome vase rather than a lot of small ones dotted about the room. She hits on the use of crumpled wire netting, though she complicates it unnecessarily by having the stuff mounted on a wooden frame. She raids the kitchen garden, finding scarlet carrot leaves in autumn, and she devotes a whole chapter to wild flowers and other material from the woods and hedgerows, including ferns and berries, and the beautiful wild clematis which everyone nowadays calls Old Man's Beard, though she and Constance give it the prettier name of Traveller's Joy.

It is the photographic illustrations – there are fifty-six of them – which give Miss Jekyll away. When it comes to actually doing the flowers, she hits it lucky once or twice, as anyone with such good material was bound to do, but for the rest she does them like we all did them in the days before Constance Spry.

Partly the trouble lies in her containers, which for all her avoidance of shirking are frequently unsuitable. Most of them are jugs, and it requires a very great skill to keep flowers in a jug from looking stodgy. Her recommended alternatives are the Chinese ginger-jar and the Indian brass lotah, shapes which might be called anti-flower, so utterly inimical are their broad shoulders and narrow mouths to any form of arrangement, (Brass vases of this shape had inhibited flower arrangers in churches for a century). And rightly deploring the ugly vases and jardinieres on sale in the shops of her day, she herself designs a series of 'Munstead glasses', and has them executed at a glass-blower's in the City.

Now that Edwardiana rank as antiques, I daresay Munstead glasses are due for rediscovery by the collectors, in which case I trust that any which have survived will be regarded merely as ornaments in their own right. One or two of the shapes are passable for flowers, but in general they are no improvement on what Miss Jekyll was already using. (The beautiful glass tazza with paeonies and clematis opposite page 25 of the book is not a 'Munstead'.)

Thus handicapped, she struggles in vain to achieve the up-soaring and down-flowing effects of the Dutch painters. She will set two vases, a larger and a smaller, side by side and hope they form a composition, but of course they merely look like a hen and chick. She will lay a trail of flowers on the table at the foot of a tall vase; the Dutch painter does that too, but his flowers, being of paint, are unfading; it is strange that a gardener like Miss Jekyll could bear to see real flowers gasping like fish out of water. The outline of most of the arrangements is either broomstick, or cabbage.

With respect – and respect is always called for in discussing the great Gertrude Jekyll – one may say that she knew all about flower arrangement, except how to do it. The relative failure of one so gifted proves, I think, that Constance was a genuine originator, and makes good her friend Beverley Nichols' claim that we can talk of a pre-Spry and a post-Spry era. The clues Miss Jekyll left were taken up by Constance, and trans-lated in terms of her own vision. Just as the Dutch painter had seen in his mind's eye a construction of flowers that had never existed, so Constance saw one; only she found the way to make it come true.

Yet had Miss Jekyll shared Constance's passion for junk-shops, she could have found, and in greater quantity than Constance a generation later, the containers that made Con-stance's arrangements possible. They were objects finely fashioned by previous ages, mostly for other purposes than that of holding flowers. They were the porcelain or marble urns which formed part of mantel-piece garnitures, a pair often flanking a clock. They were marble tazzas brought back from the Grand Tour. They were pottery vegetable dishes and fruit comports. They were big stone vases from the garden, or lesser ones from the terrace or the conservatory. Even the despised brass or silver epergne, against which Miss Jekyll railed, might, dismantled into its component parts, have furnished her with miniature vases more attractive than a lotah or a ginger-jar.

The genius, inherited from her mother, which Constance had for junk-shopping has been commented on by all who knew her; there was about it something uncanny. Travelling on top of a bus to Homerton, she would spy an object in an East End pawnbroker's or old-clothes shop, and out she would get at the next stop, and go back, and probably acquire yet another treasure. Marjorie Fletcher or Josephine Cook, as they drove her about on business, would be constantly stopped: 'I've seen something.' It was usually filthy and in their eyes unpromising, but Constance's had taken in a good shape. 'Never mind,' she would say, 'wait till I've got it cleaned up.' And then it might turn out to be copper or alabaster; but even if it were base metal, she could find a use for it because the shape was satisfying. She was never frightened of the really enormous vase, in wood or stone. Lond before she had a shop, she maintained that they would come in one day; and come in they did.

There was a handsome profit to be made from re-selling such finds, and throughout the years, off and on, she did so, but always reluctantly. They were an essential part of her equipment and inspiration. For the shop, for re-sale and as decorators' vases, what she needed was inexpensive pottery in good shapes and white or pale colours, and it was virtually impossible to find. She was reduced to treating ordinary brown jugs with white paint (this was still being done when Sheila Macqueen joined the firm three years later, and the jugs were still selling as fast as the staff could paint them.) For the boat-shaped vases that were needed on mantelpieces, and for wall vases, Flo Standfast would make her up shapes in papiermâché, which were then varnished or coated with plaster. Later, Miss Standfast modelled the designs in clay and they were executed in modest quantities by the Fulham Pottery. If any of these early Spry pieces have survived on pantry shelves, their owners may be interested to know that collectors are now looking out for them.

When she went out decorating to customers' houses, Constance found interiors and possessions of great beauty, for she was working now for wealthy people who justified their wealth by using it with taste, otherwise they would not have called in an obscure florist from the wilds of Pimlico. Either from the Atkinson windows, or from seeing her work in a friend's house, they recognized that she was doing what they had been groping towards themselves. Some found her by a happy accident; thus, Lady Portarlington was driving home after a Royal Horticultural Society show when she saw the window of the little shop and something exquisite standing in it. She stopped her car, went in and asked for the owner, and so started a friendship which was to be lifelong.

But at first, even these clients offered her the conventional cut-glass vases and silver rose-bowls, and there was some blenching when she asked if she might use instead the heir-looms she saw around her, the fine pieces in bronze and marble, the old silver or silver-gilt cups (shiny modern silver she never could abide), or if it were for a dinner-party, the tureen sand sauceboats of the service, so much more graceful than the table vases of the time. Once the experiment had been tried, they were delighted, and the heirloom, perhaps scarcely glanced at for years, took on a new life.

Constance learned much from these early patrons, as she took in the quality of each room and planned to emphasize it by her flowers. Sir Francis and Lady Oppenheimer in Vincent Square were artists in their own right, he a talented flower painter, and the garden of their country house was full of new ideas. Lady Portarlington had one of the first all-white interiors in London, and she had not called in the fashionable Syrie Maugham to create it for her but had designed it herself. She agreed that her magnificent collection of celadon vases should be used, and it was possible to build breathtaking groups against these ivory walls – eucalyptus, green hydrangea heads, lichened branches, white lilies, with perhaps one brilliant spike of a scarlet anthurium. Wilkinson's pretty scent-shop was a setting for charm, but rooms like this, with every object in them superb, were settings for grandeur, and it was grandeur that brought Constance's talent out to the full. The fact that any money she liked could be spent on the flowers was helpful, but not essential. Outline, scale and setting were what mattered. She writes somewhere of 'laurel, arranged by itself, grandly'. If the container and the background were right, prunings from the shrubbery would do.

Flowers must suit not only the room but the occasion. Constance was the first to realize what now seems so obvious, that for a dance or large party, which means a roomful of people standing up, it is useless to have the flowers lower than eye-level. The conventional florist banked them on the floor and for preference in the empty fireplace, a trick she particularly disliked. She strove by every means to raise them aloft – hence the value of mantelpiece flowers, arranged, *faute de mieux,* in a series of linked bread-tins which could then be disguised. Hence flowers on bookcases, tallboys, any high piece of furniture. Best of all were pedestals, which the grand house could usually supply, even if it meant looking in the attics, for there had been a Victorian vogue for pedestals bearing downflowing house plants. Anything that might make a pedestal was bought in her junkshop rounds; later she had pedestals made of plywood, painted white and picked out in gilt; later still the making of wrought-iron pedestals, painted black or white, gave a new and agreeable employment to the more artistic village blacksmiths. But in the first years it was still a question of improvising with whatever one could find.

By the end of the first summer, it was obvious that Constance must have an assistant, though difficult to see how she could possibly find time to train one. She went to an agency, one which specialized in finding girls of good education. Never again did she need to use an agency; there were always more young people longing to work for her, or be apprenticed to her, than she could take. But on this unique occasion, the Fletcher luck was in working order. The young woman sent by the agency proved to have natural good taste, efficiency, loyalty and a clear business head, qualities which were to make her the ideal second-in-command.

Valerie Pirie came of an old Franco-Scottish family. Her grandfather, having married a Frenchwoman, discovered that she could not live happily away from her native soil. Accordingly he bought the Château de Varennes, near Angers, and

<<<<<<<<<<<<<<<<<<<<<<<<<<<<<<<<<<<<<<<<<<<<<<<<<<<

10. As hundreds remember her. Holding a weekend course for housewives in the main drawing-room at Winkfield.

11. 'Now where shall I put it?' The clutter of decorative objects is typical of Constance's flair.

transported himself and his family, his flocks and herds and possessions, by boat from Aberdeen and up the Loire to his new property. The Pirie girls spoke French as their first language until the outbreak of the 1914–18 war, when their father joined up and their mother brought them to England.

When she left school Val Pirie had hopes of becoming a concert pianist, and studied for a time under Solomon, but then decided that she lacked the necessary talent. Her flair for fashion and elegance suggested a career in dressmaking as an alternative, and she was apprenticed to a very tough London woman couturier, and treated as runabouts in such establishments always were – rather like a probationer in a hospital or a novice in a nunnery. It was, she says, a salutary discipline, and she learned a good deal about the realities of the smart shopping world, but the prospect at the far end of all these snubs and scoldings hardly seemed to compensate.

She went back to the agency which had found her the job, and was told of a small florist who wanted someone interested in flowers and gardening and able to drive a small van. She was dubious, the pay was only £2 10s. weekly, less than she had been getting, and though she loved the garden at Varennes she only knew the names of the flowers in French. An interview with Constance reassured her on all points. She knew that this was where she wanted to work.

Val Pirie vividly remembers her first day at 7 Belgrave Road, in September of 1929. She arrived at eight on a Monday morning, which seemed to her an exemplary time to report for shop duty, and found a frantic Flo Standfast on the pavement exclaiming: 'Mrs Spry's in the Market, she expected you at six!' She leapt into the van and drove hell for leather to Covent Garden, to find another anxious little figure on the pavement, surrounded by boxes and baskets. Her apologies were waved aside: 'Just get me to Atkinsons in Bond Street,' said Mrs Spry.

The boxes were unpacked, and Constance set to work on one of the big soapstone urns, saying to Val, 'you do the other to match.' With trembling fingers Val did her beginner's best, and presently Constance came over and thanked and praised, and slightly retouched. It was the mysterious technique of

teaching without seeming to, whereby she was to train all the
early recruits to the decorating side, though not under quite
such harassing conditions.

Working with her was delightfully warm and friendly. One
was treated as a colleague, not as a learner. It was never 'wait
till I show you'; ideas and initiative were encouraged, and if,
as happened at first, the results were not quite up to the Spry
standard, there was always praise first and criticism afterwards. It was also exceedingly strenuous as a way of life, from
the Market at six in the morning till the shop closed at six in
the evening – or later, if there were a party to do.

Soon Val Pirie found herself happy to spend most of her
weekends at Abinger, relishing the semi-wild garden, the
rambling old house, the good food, the lively and far-ranging
talk of Shav Spry and Constance; but also putting in a hard
Sunday afternoon's work picking, in the garden, the woods
and the hedgerows. A huge hamper of background material,
leaves or bare branches, went up to town with them on Mondays. On her first week-end, she and Spry were sent out by
Constance with instructions to find branches of larch well
studded with cones. Neither of them dared confess that they
were not sure which were larches among the many conifers
of the Abinger woods. Fortunately, instinct guided them right.

She quickly got the feel of the Market, the plan being that
she should take over the buying from Constance, as indeed she
did for a time, before handing over in her turn to George
Foss. Constance herself loved Covent Garden, and always kept
her eye in by visits from time to time. And in those days,
ironically enough, it was a far more exciting place than it
became after the war, with a big flower-arranging movement
alert for rarities. Even this demand does not, it seems, make it
viable to grow rarities commercially any longer, and George
Foss prophesies that soon there will not be more than eight or
nine sorts of flowers grown for sale – starting with Constance's
bête noire, the chrysanthemum all-the-year-round.

Her favourite haunt was the French Department, into which
Mediterranean flowers and plants came in the early part of the
year: branches of eucalyptus, palm, pepper-tree; the flat bam-
boo baskets with lids called 'pads', packed tightly with tube-

roses or lilies of the valley, or the black and green Mourning Iris, or huge Parma violets. Traders quickly learned that if they had anything new and strange, an orchid, an anthurium, a passion flower, the likeliest customer was Mrs Spry.

She was something new to the Market. She amused and delighted them, but nobody took her seriously at first. 'I give you a fortnight,' an official of the Covent Garden Authority said. She outlived the fortnight, but when George Foss took over, and met buyers from the old-established florists in the breakfast room which the great Garden firm of Munro ran as a favour to its customers, he was still being told 'you won't last another year'.

Basil Unite, the present head of Munro's, was then a young man who had just completed his training and taken over the lily department. He remembers his surprise when Constance first walked into his office. The Market was hardly a lady's world, but there she stood, humming with vitality, 'like a little transistor set that you tuned into immediately.' And although she was a modest customer by Munro's standards, her influence made itself felt. She insatiably wanted white lilies and white arums; he got Mrs James de Rothschild to grow extra quantities for her. She wanted big branches of magnolia and camellia and species rhododendrons, and suchlike slow-growing shrubs; these had already been arriving in small quantities from the only source that could provide them, mature private gardens of the last century, whose owners were now glad to help defray their garden expenses by selling the prunings. With the coming of Constance, this traffic greatly increased. Material was sent by Sheffield Park and Exbury, by Caerhays and Tresco and other Cornish gardens; today, though less publicized than the seasonal daffodils, it is a steady, year-round trade.

The buying completed and the much-needed breakfast consumed, Constance and Val would load up the little green Austin van. It had a canvas carrier on the roof, and the load of branches would protrude fore and aft. Then they sped back along the Embankment. The policeman on duty at Westminster Bridge got to know the van with its thatch of green, and would hold up the traffic to let them pass.

Then the real work of the day began. There were three main

bread-and-butter jobs when Val Pirie joined 'Flower Decorations'; Atkinsons' windows, done on Mondays but visited daily in case anything needed renewing; four big windows in Drage's furniture shop in Tottenham Court Road, tricky because they were hot and flowers tended to wilt; and the distribution and arrangement of pot plants in the foyers of four Granada Cinemas, a task involving hard physical labour. In addition there was the steadily increasing flow of commissions from private customers for parties, dances and weddings.

The weddings, rewarding both aesthetically and financially, presented a problem to the florist new in London, as indeed they still do, because the handful of fashionable wedding churches only allow three or four established florists inside their doors, and these, naturally, tend to be the old-established ones. But Lady Emily Lutyens, wife of the eminent architect, was planning the wedding of her daughter Mary in St Margarets, Westminster, in February of 1930, and being already an appreciative customer, she wished Constance to decorate it. St Margarets were most unwilling. 'You can't blame them,' Val Pirie says, 'after all we were just a back-street florist.' But Lady Emily, a woman of immense personality backed up by her husband's prestige, held firm.

Constance's ideas for wedding decoration, and for church decoration generally, were as original as her ideas for parties and had developed from them. A church, she said, should not look like a conservatory – which was more or less how the conventional florist did make it look, with great banks of potted plants and palms at floor level. (It was said that the favourite palms of the leading florists could have found their way into St Margarets or St Georges Hanover Square by themselves.) The beautiful features of a church should be left unadorned, and if there were ugly ones they should not be camouflaged, but the eye distracted by the old conjuror's trick of putting interest somewhere else. Constance advocated two large flower-arrangements on tall pedestals, one each side of the chancel steps, with further flowers on the altar if desired. Today, the simplest village wedding is decorated in this manner. It is hard to realize that she evolved it, and that my generation can remember, as children, helping to 'do the church' for

Christmas or Easter by twining greenery round pillars and pulpit and font, just as Trollope's Lily Dale was doing in the 1860s.

Mary Lutyens herself, with commendable imagination, had decided to play up the wintry aspect of the season; her dress and those of her bridesmaids were to be in ice-blue satin, the pageboys in blue velvet tabards and carrying silver trumpets. St Margarets was persuaded to put down a blue carpet in place of the traditional red one. As for the flowers, February is not the easiest month; nor was there unlimited money to spend.

Constance and Val Pirie found in the Market huge branches of a particularly beautiful eucalyptus, *E. globulus*, with white seed-heads. They sat up half the night painting the backs of the leaves blue. The branches were then arranged in urns on alabaster pedestals and they looked like two waterfalls, cascading on either side of the chancel steps. The effect was exquisite and quite unlike anything that had been seen at a wedding before. The event attracted much newspaper publicity, of which the 'flowers' had their full share. After this triumph, it was not possible for any of the smart churches to refuse Constance entry. As with accounts at good shops, when you had none you could not have one, but when you had one you could have them all.

The commissions piled up, and more staff had urgently to be found. And again, the luck that seemed always to attend Constance in her appointments sent her people who were to be allies for life. She felt that it would be useful and pleasant to have a man about the place; George Foss, at twenty-four, came with an introduction from Drage's, where his brother worked. He was a country boy from the New Forest, whose ambition was to become a head gardener, but his father had pronounced that they were a dying race, and put him into stationery, where he was unhappy and bored. He jumped at the chance to become a Covent Garden buyer, and to handle flowers and plants. He could not drive, but that was no impediment; Val Pirie put him into the van and made him drive round and round Vincent Square till he ran into a lamp-post, after which he was considered qualified.

With him, the little shop gained an element of stability, humour and masculine resourcefulness which was wholly welcome. He was willing to turn his hand to anything, or if it was beyond him, to find precisely the chap to do it; making tin linings for Constance's innumerable vase finds, converting Bible boxes and occasional tables to hold plants, constructing pedestals, screens and backgrounds. He accepted with amusement his position as, for some years, the only man in a small feminine world, was infinitely kind and helpful to the beginners, and always had a shoulder for anyone to weep on. The acquisition in due course of a charming wife and daughter gave him a home life in peaceful contrast to the febrile atmosphere of the shop. But they were never allowed to do the flowers.

For like almost all those who joined Constance, he presently found that he too had a decorating talent, and when he could be spared from other duties, loved to exercise it. (Only her successive secretaries seemed able to resist this itch to have a go.) He was to develop into one of the most successful lecturers and demonstrators the movement has produced, and not the least of his services has been to prove that it is no more unsuitable for his sex to enjoy arranging flowers than to enjoy growing them.

The two other acquisitions, secured when a West End florist gave up, were Miss White as head florist and Miss Oldfield as head saleswoman. Constance's requirements in floristry were exacting; it must look like jewellery, and she called it 'ironmongery' if any wiring showed. 'Whitey' was in fact a jeweller's daughter and her work had a jeweller's precision; she could take on incredibly delicate tasks like wiring separately each bell of a bunch of hyacinths to form a wedding spray; it was largely thanks to her skill that Constance was able to evolve crescent-shaped sprays instead of broomstick bunches for brides to carry.

Miss Oldfield was a large, calm and dignified lady who knew all the arts of a saleswoman, as, for example, how to present a specimen bouquet for the inspection of bride and mother: always bring it in swathed in tissue paper, and unveil it with a flourish. She was dubious about exchanging Dover

Street for a shop on the wrong side of the tracks; she had always been West End, she said. Perhaps it was hinted to her that with a little patience, she would presently be West End again.

An assistant was also found for Flo Standfast, whose perfectly fashioned flowers of waxed paper were built up into 'Flemish pictures', sold at what then seemed high prices, and kept by the customer till they looked dusty; with care they were still beautiful after two years. (It is a pity the Victorian fashion for glass domes had not survived to protect them, for they too would be collectors' pieces now). In addition Miss Standfast made flower and shell jewellery, and to her fell the honour of first drawing Royal attention to the shop's work.

Constance had met at a lunch party Lady Dawson, wife of the royal physician (not yet a peer). There was a dinner invitation from the Palace, for which tiaras were regulation wear; Lady Dawson, as a mere doctor's wife, did not own one and disliked the idea of hiring. 'Let us make you something,' said Constance, and bore her back to Belgrave Road. She evolved and Flo Standfast carried out a design of tiny full-blown roses and rosebuds, made entirely from pale pink shells. At the dinner, it caught the eye of King George v, to whom real diamond tiaras were no novelty. He came over to Lady Dawson and remarked in his gruff naval way: 'That's a very pretty thing you have on your head.'

Inevitably, as Constance's reputation grew, she was taken up by women who wished to patronize her not only as a flower decorator, but as a person. She was always very wary of thus combining business with social life. She was a shopkeeper, she would say, and shopkeepers do not attend the customer's parties. She hardly ever accepted dinner invitations, being, indeed, weary at the end of her long day, and only anxious to spend a quiet evening with her adored Shav. But with the encouragement of her staff she occasionally went to lunch parties; she made useful contacts, and saw her flowers 'in action' as it were, and this, they felt, was important. And in congenial company she would keep everyone laughing with her stories and mimicry, but it was always an effort to her to meet strangers. Perhaps shyness had always underlain her youthful vivacity; it certainly increased with the years.

However, the summons that reached Constance from Syrie Maugham was not a social one, but very much *de haut en bas,* the great lady summoning the florist. Syrie Maugham was a shopkeeper, quite as much as Constance, but she had no notion of being treated like one. Her attitude of condescension did not outlast the meeting. They were instantly friends and allies; as with Wilkinson, there was an instinctive sympathy of feeling and taste.

Mrs. Somerset Maugham, the improbable daugher of an eminent philanthropist, had come a long way since her school-mates knew her as Queenie Barnardo; through two marriages, the second of which might well have been considered a judg-ment on her for abandoning the first, and through the disaster of loving a man who should never have married anybody, and whose talents enabled him to lampoon and vilify her for the rest of their lives. Tough and resilient, she had turned her own gifts to interior decorating, and evolved the all-white Baroque style which Mr Osbert Lancaster was to satirize – but kindly – as 'Vogue Regency'. It was not only clean, elegant and an ad-mirable setting for heirlooms; it was also wildly impractical, in a London which had not yet enforced smoke abatement. (Sig-nificantly, it never caught on in the northern cities.) Rooms needed redecorating once a year, upholstery had to be washed or dry-cleaned once a month. Far from detracting, this added to its appeal; it was an outward and visible sign of wealth. And like all fashions, it was copied right down the financial scale. We of the under-privileged classes sat on grimy porridge-coloured sofas for years.

This passion for white, and for Baroque objects, was Con-stance's also, and she had no difficulty in convincing Mrs Maugham that white flowers were the ideal complement to a white room, their infinite gradations of green or cream standing out against white walls, with the right lighting, almost as if sculptured. The difficulty was to convince the customers, so deeply was the tradition ingrained that white flowers were for funerals. For this purpose lilies and arums were grown by

several specialist nurserymen, who were astonished at an increase in their trade beyond what the demands of mortality
would warrant, as London society gradually capitulated to the
campaign of Mrs Somerset Maugham and Mrs Spry.

In her first book, *Flower Decoration*, Constance lovingly
describes the pleasure of working for Syrie Maugham, the
beauty of her Chelsea house with its huge white salon and pine-
panelled dining-room, the pieces of old Chelsea and other
ornaments, any of which could be used for flowers, and her
open and experimental mind. She knew nothing about flowers
except what she wanted, liked colours to be either muted or
brilliant, as in nasturtiums or 'pegaloniums' (her floral mala-
propisms were a constant joy to Constance), and for her
daughter's coming-out party had one room decorated with wild
fireweed, which looked exquisite and gave far more trouble
than conventional flowers would have done.

Syrie Maugham was a tough nut, but after all she had need
to be. She was liked and respected, both by her own work-
people and by Constance's, and that is a fair test of an em-
ployer's equality. She demanded the best, but was generous and
appreciative in her acknowledgment of it. At the time of this
coming-out party Constance was on holiday with her friends
the Hensons in Hammamet, and the work devolved on a team
under Val Pirie. Not only were they suitably thanked and rewarded, but a telegram of description and praise was sent to
Constance in Tunisia. Such incidents are remembered.

Commercially, her support was extremely valuable. She was
the smartest interior decorator in London, and wealthy clients
were continually urged to have Mrs Spry put the finishing
touches to the rooms she had created for them. But Constance's affection for her was not based on mutual gain; none
of her affections were. They met as fellow artists, and it was a
feeling that endured.

More of a patroness and less of a colleague was Mrs Wilfrid
Ashley, the formidable stepmother of Edwina Mountbatten
(who detested her). Mistress both of Broadlands and of a superb
London house, for which she had designed a staircase with
alternate risers of black and white marble (a stumbling-block
for those who had dined too well), she was a domineering

woman, and no great favourite with the staff at Belgrave Road. But she had a genuine decorating talent, and this, far more than the money she spent, the customers she introduced and the shows of Flo Standfast's work that she held, caused her to become Constance's friend.

She did not, of course, soil her hands with actual gardening, (she is said to have been the first person in London to paint her fingernails), but she was a knowledgeable garden designer, and under her direction the gardens at Broadlands attained a beauty they had not known before. She broke away from the 'blaze of colour' border to which most English gardeners were still addicted, and planned her borders in harmonizing tones, one blue and grey, one all-red, one silver and white. Ten men gardeners were employed, and two girls; the girls were a series of students, just down from Studley Horticultural College, who shared a bothy in the grounds and were paid very little, it being understood that they were receiving a training in gracious gardening – as indeed they were. Not the least of Molly Ashley's contributions to Constance's progress was to have handed on to her, ready trained, two of her best decorators, Margaret Watson and Joyce Robinson.

The girls did light garden work like dead-heading in the middle of the week, but their chief job was to pick and arrange flowers for the large week-end house-parties. The house was decorated with the same sure eye for colour; each room had its complement of matching vases and the flowers had to tone. The saloon was copper and orange; one drawing-room was in the colours of old English and Dresden china, another had a plum carpet and green walls and the flowers would be in yellow, purple and puce; the study had a red embossed paper and the flowers would be red or white, or sometimes 'clashing reds'. Both the colour combinations and the methods of arrangement were very like Constance's, and may have been directly copied from her. Certainly Joyce Robinson, who was an occupant of the bothy in 1930, remembers much talk of this wonderful new friend in London and the things she was doing, and the girls would make up bunches of flowers to be taken back to Mrs Spry on Mondays. But when finally Mrs Spry herself was prevailed on to come down to Broadlands, she in her turn was amazed by its beauty and the lavishness of its scale. Probably this, too, was a two-way traffic in ideas.

Both Margaret Watson and Joyce Robinson look back with a wry respect at Mrs Ashley, much as nurses look back on a tough but knowledgeable matron. They learnt from her elements of sophisticated decor which they could hardly, at that time, have acquired in any other way. And she was not always an ogress; there were moments when she laughed at herself. 'Exit tornado', she would say as she got into her car after the week-end, knowing full well that she left behind her gasps of relief.

In comparison with this millionaire establishment, the commission which reached Constance from the wife of another distinguished architect was modest, but it was one after her heart. Mrs Edward Maufe had also trained as an architect, specializing in decoration, and she persuaded Sir Ambrose Heal to let her furnish a show flat in the Mansard Gallery of his shop, then an idea quite novel to London. (Her own family were shocked at the prospect of her working in a shop, even though she did not actually sell anything; it is strange to think that such prejudices persisted into the 1930s.) To give the flat a lived-in look, a weekly vase of flowers was ordered from Mrs Spry.

'It was a weekly masterpiece,' says Lady Maufe, 'and I used to look forward to meeting a genius every Monday.' Word spread among the Heal customers, and some of them began to pay weekly visits also, not so much to see the furniture which was for sale, as to see the flowers which were not.

Lady Maufe further remembers, as many do, being disappointed by her first sight of Mrs Spry. She had pictured someone tall and elegant as her own lilies; instead arrived this short, and by now plump, middle-aged woman, wearing an overall and an outsized hat and with an armload of incongruously jangling bracelets. One's impression was of a fussy little dowager duchess; but it did not survive the fascination of watching her swift hands at work, nor, once she had got over her shyness, the good fun of her talk.

But the picture certainly does not square with the elegance of her Dublin photographs, nor with the 'flamboyant' dressing that had won young Homerton's heart. Her clothes were always beautifully made, but she had ceased to take much interest in them, and though she would put on an elaborate outfit for a platform appearance, the shop's working overalls, designed by herself through the years, give a far happier impression of her personality. In Homerton, she had dressed to give the children 'something pretty to look at'. Now she gave Mayfair her flowers instead.

The year 1931 was one of moving house. First, the lease of Abinger Rectory fell in, and Constance and Shav, still wanting a country way of life, moved to Colney Park, near Aldenham. House and garden were both on the grand scale, and the garden had been planted by a connoisseur; to come continually on new treasures in the way of shrubs was to Constance a delight. It was less delightful to Walter Trower, who found himself running single-handed a garden which had formerly had a staff of three. At near-by Aldenham Court was an even more notable garden, belonging to the Hon. Vicary Gibbs, who had collected plants from all over the world, and also ran a nursery. The nursery was being given up, and at the closing-down sale Constance attended on the first day, and made Walter attend all the others, for experience.

They acquired many rarities, including magnolias and *Descaisnia fargesii*, but the best purchase was a stock of snow-berries, much more thickly clustered with white berries than the type. The admiration of visitors revealed to Constance that she had found a unique clone, and it was eventually marketed by the Sunningdale Nurseries as *Symphoricarpus* 'Constance Spry'. She was touchingly pleased by the honour. The plant by which her name is now better known, the hybrid 'old' rose 'Constance Spry', was only evolved by Mr David Austin after her death.

A further source of supply, both for garden and for shop, was the shows of the Royal Horticultural Society, of which Constance was a keen supporter. She and George Foss would attend late in the afternoon of the second day's showing, when many exhibitors sell plants off cheaply rather than have to cart them home again. They would buy, perhaps, a whole stand of lilies, the flowers would adorn the next wedding or party, and the precious bulbs would go into the borders of the large walled garden at Colney Park.

Gradually the little staff at Belgrave Road increased. Eleanor Gielgud joined as Constance's first secretary, and Joyce Robinson as a much needed additional decorator, ready trained by Mrs Ashley. And Constance, with a fraction more of time at her disposal, was able to accept an invitation to visit Swanley Horticultural College weekly, and give its students a flower-arrangement class.

Financially the fee was negligible; she could have earned, and needed to earn, much more in London. But she loved Swanley, the renewed contact with the world of education, the company of fresh-faced young girls who were intending to devote their lives to gardening, as she would have done, she always said, if she had had the chance. It was a complete break from the hothouse atmosphere of society functions. The class was small, about fifteen girls, and there was no question of a formal lecture. They wandered round the big gardens collecting material, as often as not from the vegetable garden, for shape, the girls found, mattered more to Mrs Spry than colour. Then, in the big saloon of the college, they created the outsize and lavishly flowing arrangements Constance loved, and even the least talented caught her enthusiasm. The Swanley students were indeed fortunate, for no other group, not even the learners in the flower school which she herself was to start a little later, ever got so much of Mrs Spry's personal attention.

Swanley held for her the further pleasure of contact with a first-rate botanical mind. Dr Kate Barratt, the Principal, had been a lecturer and researcher at Imperial College, and then on the staff of the Brookline Botanic Garden. Over lunch, Constance would pick her brains. She knew herself to be botanically a beginner, but she had her father's passionate desire to learn. It is significant that the connection with Swanley was kept up right through the war, and not relinquished till Dr Barratt was on the point of retirement and Constance was planning a school of her own.

Miss Gielgud, whose first job it was, started the tradition that Constance's secretaries were the only people around the place who positively did not want to arrange flowers; though she did learn to wire in her off-moments, and could help the florist out with 'violet cushions' and similar funeral accessories. Nell Gielgud brought to the business a racy tongue – most of the nicknames were coined by her – and a whiff of stage glamour. Her brother John was making his first big success as Richard of Bordeaux, and having money to spend, spent a generous amount of it on flowers for his friends, as he still does. Many of his less affluent colleagues would drop in, even if it was only to buy a single rose, and some who were 'resting' helped out on the sales side for the fun of it, and got no pay. Indeed, the firm's finances were still extremely precarious, and many a time Nell Gielgud wondered if there would be enough in the kitty to pay the salaries – or even more importantly, to pay the Covent Garden wholesalers' bills, for the Market allows no credit.

She was blithely informed by Constance that it was part of her duty to keep the books. She had had only an elementary training in book-keeping, and she was further unnerved by finding that it was often book-keeping in the red. When Shav Spry, who was invariably kind to the young women in the shop, found her weeping over the accounts, he told her that she could come down to Colney Park for two or three week-ends and he would instruct her. By this means, he made some disconcerting discoveries himself.

Only the floristry and the cut-flower sections were showing a real profit. In spite of the long hours worked by Constance, Val Pirie and George Foss and the heavy demands on their services, the decorating side barely broke even. This was mainly because Constance, in her modesty and her ignorance of costing, had made her prices far too low. For all the great vases at Atkinsons, retouched two or three times a week, she charged a mere £5, and Heal's 'weekly masterpiece' cost them a pound. Both commissions brought valuable publicity, but a small and under-capitalized business cannot live on publicity. Moreover, Constance was frequently naughty. If she suddenly decided that a group needed an orchid or lily or similar expensive addition, someone would be sent round to a rival florist's to buy it at retail price, and all the profit would be gone.

And Miss Standfast and her assistant, toiling away at their 'arts' and their Flemish groups, were incurring a serious loss. Neither Constance nor Val Pirie had the experience to realize that when you manufacture goods for sale, instead of re-selling the goods produced by others (which is basically what the florist does), the costing must be done on an altogether different basis. Shav Spry found that a creation which was priced at thirty shillings had actually cost the firm forty-two shillings' worth of Miss Standfast's time to make.

At this dismaying juncture, when retrenchment seemed the only answer, there came an invitation to further capital outlay. A shop two doors up the street from Atkinsons fell vacant. It was obviously the right setting for Constance, its window almost marching with those she was already decorating, but the rent seemed astronomical compared with that in Belgrave Road. The backing of a husband who combined a bold and generous spirit with a steady business head was once again of inestimable value to her. He knew that if she took the shop, he would have to prime her pump once again; equally, he knew that this was an opportunity she must not miss.

In fact, the risk was less than appeared. She had more work than she knew how to do, and she needed to be among those she worked for – as Syrie Maugham was, who had never made the mistake of starting at the bottom and working up. A Bond Street address would enable her to charge the same prices as those florists with whom she now competed in the importance of her commissions. It would mean a brisker sale of cut flowers, as customers passed the shop instead of having to direct their steps or their chauffeurs to Pimlico. And though not extensive, the premises were at any rate bigger than those in Belgrave Road, and would enable her to take on more staff.

Accordingly the move was made. Miss Oldfield, to her great gratification, found herself West End once more, and Constance was West End at last.

5. WEST END

Number 4 Burlington Gardens, next door to the Arcade, consisted of an elegant small showroom with offices behind, and a roomy basement, reached by a murderously steep flight of outside stairs. Shav Spry planned the new shop for more efficient working and less waste, including the installation of a big refrigerator to keep cut flowers. The Belgrave Road premises were not immediately re-let, and Constance was for allowing Miss Standfast and her assistant to remain there; Flo Standfast had always evoked her maternal protection, and was treated *en grande artiste,* to an extent which sometimes annoyed younger members of the staff. It was of no use, he pointed out, for Flo and her assistants to work as though each piece were intended for the British Museum; it might be praiseworthy, but it wasn't commercial. They needed to be under the boss's eye, and then, when necessary, she could prod.

The value of the move was immediately apparent; the four decorators were run off their feet and another was urgently needed. Good fortune sent Constance an ideal recruit. Sheila Young, with a family tradition of gardening behind her, longed for a career in flowers. She and her mother had come up to London for an interview with a school of floristry, which depressed them. Walking away down Bond Street, they saw an urn of leek seed-heads in Atkinsons' window; 'that's the sort of thing I want to do!' Sheila exclaimed, went boldly into the shop and asked who had done it, and was directed to No. 4. And Constance was persuaded to take this eager girl as an apprentice, for a monthly premium.

Nell Gielgud set her to strip sloe branches of their leaves;

she was mystified, but laboured on, till Constance's amused voice said behind her, 'You need only bother with those that have fruit.' For the next three days she painted earthenware jugs, and helped to carry completed vases about. Then Constance let her try her hand at an Atkinsons window, using what had become her standard technique for instruction: putting in two or three key branches herself and handing over with a 'now finish that'. After the first month, she told Mr Young that she would take no more premiums for his daughter. The girl had such an outstanding natural flair that she was already a valuable member of the staff.

Sheila Young, whom the flower world now knows as Sheila Macqueen, and Joyce Robinson, rechristened by Miss Gielgud 'Robbo', became in a special sense Constance's chief decorators of the 1930s. Not only did they take over from Val Pirie, who was becoming steadily more absorbed by the administration of the rapidly growing firm, and from George Foss, who had his hands full with the buying, and presently with the running of a department for the care of London gardens and window-boxes. Gradually, they took over the actual mechanics of flower arrangement from Constance herself, becoming her 'hands' – never entirely her eyes, for those she did not cease to use.

The vision remained with her and was communicated, but the doing of the things came to bore her, as anything bored her if it went on too long. She achieved better results through Sheila and Robbo than she had achieved by herself, a mysterious relationship which neither of them can explain, except by saying that she always made them feel the quality of the growing plant or flower. She kept them alert, never wishing to see the same effect twice, instantly pouncing on and dismissing a formula, sometimes seeming barely to glance at a completed group, but dropping some tiny comment like 'lime green in the middle' which made all the difference.

Today, though Robbo's life as the wife of a doctor leaves her time for only very occasional professional flower arrangement, Sheila Macqueen has gone on to become the best-known of Constance's successors, as indefatigable lecturer and demonstrator both here and in America. Her own style has evolved and simplified, her own enthusiasm has never flagged, and she is producing work which many would consider to be the most beautiful in the world. Yet it is with no false modesty, but rather with a genuine sense of loss, that she will tell you: 'I haven't had a new idea since Connie died.'

But if Constance inspired and at one remove directed them, she none the less allowed the decorators to be themselves. The pattern was consistent: a new decorator would be paired with an experienced one and would copy, producing one of a pair of matching or complementary vases, successfully for a time. Then he or she would begin to evolve a personal style, and the copying became increasingly more difficult, finally impossible. Any of the decorators, walking down Bond Street, could immediately tell which of them had done the Atkinsons windows that week.

Just how they recognized each other's stamp is, again, difficult for them to explain. George Foss comes nearest to it when he says that Sheila can be recognized by her placing of each flower to bring out its individuality, her spontaneous freshness, (another colleague says of her that 'any flowers she arranges look like springtime', and Constance herself praised her 'natural, almost casual air, far from easy to achieve.') Robbo's gift, he thinks, is for nobility and grandeur of line, which has little to do with actual size, and may be seen equally well in an arrangement of forsythia in her husband's waiting-room, and in a mammoth construction which has to compete with the Gothic splendour of Norwich Cathedral. George Foss's own interest is chiefly in movement; his are very much a gardener's flowers, just brought in from outside, and looking as if still liable to be ruffled by the breeze.

That such wide diversities of talent and temperament could express themselves through the same, and in its outlines classical, medium, is surely proof that Constance had invented not just a pretty handicraft, but a genuine minor art.

But in the Burlington Garden days, the young decorators were still, of course, very much under Constance's immediate supervision. She went with them to every new client, and she personally planned every large-scale commission, as for a dance or party. She studied each new interior: 'my first instinct is to seek some note round which to plan a scheme'. It was not difficult in the lovely houses; Lady Howard de Walden's green marble staircase in Belgrave Square could best be emphasized by mixed foliage arrangements; Mrs Ashley's onyx table lit from beneath gave a water-lily quality to any white flowers. But there were also ugly, cluttered rooms which, as she said, made her 'think with longing of what could be done with a whitewashed barn.' Her tact on these occasions was an object-lesson to the girls. Without hurting the owner's feelings, she would contrive to suggest that a curtain or swathe of fabric should be hung over the garish wallpaper or the deplorable picture, and the flowers set against it.

Mrs Spry's young ladies, as their admirers called them, had their accepted routine. They always went to the front door. They always assembled the arrangement where it was to stand, not in a pantry or scullery. They always spread dust-sheets round them and cleared up immaculately, not a leaf left. The *sur place* rule applied to church decorations too, except at St Marks North Audley Street, where there was a contrary rule forbidding it; Constance protested, but its importance as a wedding church forced her to yield.

Shav Spry had taken a good gamble; the 1930s were a propitious time for a luxury flower business to get into its stride. These were the heyday debutante years, when the rich were still very rich, still lived in their large private houses and not in flats, still gave coming-out dances for their daughters in their own homes. 'We had money, and we spent it,' a famous hostess wistfully recalls.

Plenty of women would spend five or ten pounds a week on ordinary flowers for the house, or anything from fifty to five hundred pounds on flowers for a dance or wedding – and this at 1930s' money values. Sometimes these events were in country houses, to which Constance and her team would journey and stay the night; they might be treated as guests, or they might be relegated to the butler's pantry, in which case the company was often more amusing. One of these occasions is still gleefully remembered, when the hostess who had treated them *de haut en bas* had the mortification of seeing her guests fall with cries of joy upon Constance and not upon herself.

It was a customer with a fine garden in Sussex who diffidently made the suggestion that some of her own material should be used – diffidently, because she was aware that the florist's profit chiefly comes from the difference between the wholesale and retail price of flowers. Constance, however, accepted enthusiastically; to have the run of a new garden for picking was always, to her, a pleasure. Henceforward all country-house clients were given the same opportunity. Sometimes the head gardener was less gratified than the customer, but he would soften when he realized that those doing the work were gardeners too, and knew where and how to pick.

It was a very happy period, when the business was still small enough for Constance to know most of her customers personally; and it might be said of her that all her customers were friends. If an occasional difficult one came into the shop she was treated with courtesy, and Constance would relieve her own and the staff's feelings by a little mimicry afterwards. Once and once only, the actual work was disparaged, and that was not to be endured. The owner of a grand house in Curzon Street had called in the new flower decorator, and then found that she did not care for the style and would rather have carnations with asparagus fern. Constance and her team of two immediately dismantled all the vases, piled the flowers and themselves into a taxi and drove home. Constance was white with fury. 'Any ordinary flower shop would do it for her,' she said. 'I won't. I only want to do exciting things.'

But appreciative customers, be they rich or poor, could do no wrong. If one of them decided at six to throw a party, the girls stayed till eight to get the flowers done, while their own escorts for the evening sozzled themselves glumly in some pub. Their complaints against Constance were loud till they met her, when she invariably won them round. The exception was John Stuart, who was to marry Robbo, and he took care never to meet her, and thus remained in the enjoyment of his original dislike.

The hours were long and the pay was poor, but this was the general rule in the 1930s, when the gulf between rich and poor, though not quite what it had been in Edwardian times, was still wide. University graduates, whose training in those pre-grant days had cost their parents dear, were glad to accept beginners' jobs at three and four pounds a week. If anyone had told Constance that she was exploiting her staff, she would have been horrified; she paid what she could, the business was still struggling, it was still financially touch and go. The girls got presents, perquisites, friendship, consideration. If, like Sheila Young, they lived at home, the pay was pocket money. For those who had to live on it, like Robbo whose home was a farm in Lincolnshire, it was another matter. She rented a bed-sitting-room at eight shillings a week, and still remembers it with a shudder.

The contrast between their poverty and the wealthy houses they adorned should have made Bolsheviks of them; it did nothing of the sort. None of them had any feeling of pressing their noses against the window-panes of the rich. They no more expected to be guests at the party than they expected to be brides at the wedding. What they welcomed was any good chance to display their skill, and in exercising it, they felt themselves to be receiving quite as much satisfaction as those who attended merely for pleasure. In a good many instances they were doubtless right. (For myself, reporting couture dress shows on a starter's salary of £3 10s. a week, I can remember a similar sense of contentment, almost of superiority; it was more amusing to write about the clothes than it would have been to write cheques for them. Perhaps we were a poor-spirited lot.)

The young people who worked with Constance were doing what they wanted to do, and to the young that means more than cash. She liberated them as she had liberated the children of Homerton. She worked alongside them, she produced delicious cream cakes to comfort them for missing their dinner hour. Those who stayed with her in the end reaped a financial reward also, as lecturers, demonstrators, writers of books. Those who married, as most of them did, had a profitable part-time occupation to take with them into their new circle. Nevertheless, they all look back wistfully to the days when they were young and poor and overworked, but had Constance to hold them together. 'It was like a perpetual party,' they say. 'She made everything seem such fun.'

· · · · ·

Not all customers were wealthy, and many wanted the elegance of a Spry arrangement that would also have the advantage of permanency, particularly in the winter, when flowers were dear. So did the steadily growing clientele of shops and offices. For them, Constance's 'drieds' filled the bill.

The idea of dried material for house decoration was not new; the Victorians had had their palms and pampas grass, while the immediate pre-Spry era went in heavily for 'Chinese lanterns' with honesty. Her innovation was to make big and important groups with a wide variety of shapes, colours and textures. A friend, probably Wilkinson, first pointed out to her the beauty of herbaceous borders in winter, if the seed-heads of the flowers were left uncut. She looked herself, and perceived much else: the lurid metallic colours of papery hydrangea heads thrown on to a rubbish heap, seed-heads of lilies and of the vast allium tribe, seed-heads of parsnip, carrot and angelica from the vegetable garden. She experimented with drying, pressing, preserving in a mixture of water and glycerine – this last technique having, for some reason, been hitherto confined to the relatively uninteresting leaves of beech. Gradually a large range of material was collected, from which could be constructed groups impressive in their own right.

She was not very fond of preserved flowers, except for those, like achillea or hydrangea or sedum spectabile, which preserve themselves naturally on the plant with the minimum of treatment. On the other hand, she was willing to combine fresh material with dried, particularly chrysanthemums, which she actually preferred set against dried bracken rather than against evergreen. (There is, of course, a risk that fresh will make dried look dusty unless the drying has been done superbly well, which with Constance it always was.) It goes without saying that any form of dyeing or artificial colouring was taboo.

The life of a dried group should, she considered, end on the January bonfire. But many of the customers were happy to keep it the year round. Her friends the antique dealers, for instance, found that the muted amber, silver, pink, buff and ivory of the dried bouquet perfectly complemented the soft tones of old walnut or mahogany. And Sheila Young remembers visiting private houses to cheer up the dried arrangements with chrysanthemums or hellebores, till spring came round again.

Another form of semi-permanent arrangement which greatly exercised Constance's mind was the Christmas decoration. The material coming into the Market was either the conventional evergreens, with a little variegated holly if one were lucky, or else tinsel and tawdry baubles, to be hung on twigs coated with aluminium paint 'like plumbing', as she said. None of this would do for Spry customers. The evergreens she treated with gum and glitter to give the delicate effect of hoar-frost, and for the baubles she looked abroad, chiefly to Germany and Czechoslovakia, where were to be found enchanting notions – translucent bells, for instance, which, wired on to wands, made a fine effect in the ballroom at Claridges.

These were supplemented by other baubles, designed by Constance, carried out by Miss Standfast and 'the arts', and known generically as the Christmas Nonsense, though it was a nonsense taken seriously. All who knew Constance remember her busy little hands, twisting up bits of wire and velvet and silver tissue and producing some exquisite object no one else could have thought of; her flow of ideas seemed inexhaustible. The new materials as they were invented were tried out for their possibilities, the cellophanes, the plastics. From her first American trip she brought back 'the most marvellous stuff, my dears, you've never seen anything like it – ' it was Scotch tape.

The three months before Christmas became the most strenuous period in the shop's year. Parcels of the 'nonsense' went out all over the country, and the last ones would be put on the night trains at Euston or Kings Cross on Christmas Eve, while the staff wondered when, if ever, their own Christmas would begin.

The other highlight was the Chelsea Flower Show. Constance was an exhibitor from the Burlington Gardens period onwards, and she never ceased to voice her gratitude to the Royal Horticultural Society for making possible 'this great floral festival'. Of course it brought her customers, and the sort of gardener-customers she liked best, but its chief value was to keep her in touch with the world of horticulture, to which she always felt herself to belong, far more than to floristry. She loved the camararderie of the great marquee, the chance to meet growers and hybridists, the chance to see new plants and flowers, new tulips particularly. Hers was certainly a talent for all seasons, but if one season more than another is associated with her, it is that moment when spring turns to summer, the time of late tulips and first roses and of irises and lilac, the time of Chelsea.

Her own stand was kept to unfussy outlines and pale colours, in contrast to the somewhat fun-fair effect of most of the exhibits in 'Sundries Avenue'. The groups were mainly in the grand manner that suited her temperament, with her growing collection of noble alabaster urns much in evidence. (Customers sometimes asked why there were not more groups of living-room size, and she grew a trifle weary of pointing out that they would be all but invisible to the Chelsea crowd.) One vase was usually white and green, with lilies and anthuriums or magnolia, and there were vases in the soft pinks and mauves of lilac and iris, azalea and fruit blossom. But every year she thought of something new; once the centrepiece was an old gilt font from which cascaded a mass of maidenhair fern, an object-lesson in how to use material so often misused.

She has described the agonies of planning for Chelsea, how there never seemed to be an idea in her head, and how her imagination did not start to work till George Foss opened the door of his van with a flourish, and produced his special finds from the Market or Sheffield Park or Exbury. But to all who worked with her, the flow of ideas seemed to be continuous, from one Chelsea to the next.

'She never looked back,' one is told of Constance; like most artists, she was more interested in what she was to do next than in what she had just done. Sometimes the staff would be disappointed, when she returned from some big assignment, to find she could scarcely answer their questions about how it had gone. And more than one newcomer to decorating, worn out with the nervous strain of getting the Chelsea stand ready, heard the words '*Next* year I know what we'll do –' and collapsed in tears.

. . . . . .

She never looked back, never, as far as anyone remembers, revisited Homerton, though a chance encounter with a former pupil always pleased her; but of course she did not on that account forget the very different world in which she had spent half her life, or the instinctive joy that flowers brought to people who were not Mayfair hostesses. 'I do so strongly feel that flowers should be a means of self-expression for every one,' she was to write; and she strongly resented the suggestion that the grandeur of her style fitted it only for the houses and purses of the rich.

She had invented her art and wished to make it widely known, and the obvious means was a book. But she was diffident about her capacity for writing, till encouraged by a very distinguished gardener, Sir William Lawrence, sometime treasurer of the Royal Horticultural Society. He had seen and liked her work and sought her out, and thereafter gave her valuable horticultural guidance. He read her manuscript, and wrote for it a charming and percipient foreword, in which he claimed that she had 'precipitated an aesthetic renaissance'. She called the book *Flower Decoration*, and it was brought out by Dent in the spring of 1934. This began a connection which was to endure very happily for the rest of her life, and Dent's managing director, W. G. Taylor, became another valuable friend.

Henceforward she always had a book on the stocks. She never needed to repeat herself; the ideas flowed as easily in print as they did in the work-room, and her standard steadily improved; her last book, *Favourite Flowers*, is her best. By comparison this first one is beginner's work, a trifle stiff still, and with elements of the textbook. She is much influenced by Mrs Earle, but still diffident about obtruding herself or exploring by-ways; she does not yet put in the recipes and the snatches of poetry, but they will be a great improvement on Mrs Earle's when she does.

Even so, the book is far ahead of anything that had yet been written on the subject – or, for that matter, of much that has been written since; so many of the present-day flower books use vulgarisms, 'position' as a verb, 'home' continually for house, and suchlike, that set one's teeth on edge. Constance uses words fastidiously, as befits George Fletcher's daughter. She avoids the coyness which it is so difficult to keep out of writing on feminine subjects; she is friendly without ceasing to be dignified. She looks not just at the flowers and their vase but at the setting, she takes the reader into beautiful rooms which flowers can enhance, and into some ugly ones which flowers can mitigate. A design for living emerges, an encouraging conviction that there can be an artist in every family.

The principles of her art are already here: her dislike of 'tame' flowers and *déjà-vu* combinations, her preference for a single large group over several small ones, and for colour in bold patches rather than in single dots; her stress on outline, and on the need for a few flowers of massive shape to draw the eye to the centre, her resentment of set rules (though she could not foresee how much this was to be reinforced by future developments), her insistence on keeping always a receptive mind and a seeing eye. 'It is a good game to walk round the garden challenging oneself, that is to say, choosing subjects beautiful in themselves but not apparently suitable for use in vases, and picturing how they might be used. I have learned about cabbages and curly-kale, but so far turnip-tops and spring greens have defeated me.'

She writes as a gardener; not to the same extent as in later books, in which there will be more about gardening than about flower arrangement, but still, with a feeling for the growing plant, and a tacit admission that her style needs the resources of a garden behind it, though not necessarily a large one. And there is advice for the unfortunates who must rely on the florist, such as how to collect wild material from the hedges when they make trips to the country. There is no element in her books of propaganda for the sort of society florist she had become; if they bring trade, it is rather to the seedsman and the nurseryman. And indeed, this was resented by her fellow-florists, who for a long time were shortsighted enough to believe that Mrs Spry's 'cult of weeds' was bad for business.

The flowers in this first book are grouped by colours, the decorator's way; in future books it will always be by seasons, the gardener's. Of course she puts in a strong plea for her beloved all-white groups, particularly in white rooms. 'If I could choose a background for them, with the sole purpose of setting forth their intrinsic beauty, I should have a white-washed wall. Against this background the subtle gradations of colour are clearly seen. The variation in the texture of petals is one of the chief delights of white flowers, and this delicate beauty should be considered when arranging and placing them.' The point is reinforced by a reproduction of her friend Gluck's flower painting, 'Chromatic'. (In fact, this was entirely arranged by Val Pirie, who says that to her eye it now looks lumpish, and that she would do it quite differently today.)

The other illustrations are black and white photographs, except for the frontispiece, a colour reproduction of de Heem's 'Flowers in a Glass with Fruit,' from which she draws many lessons. She was rightly suspicious of colour photography in its early stages, though the alternative adopted in later books, of photographs coloured by hand, was not a happy one. Only towards the end of her life did colour photographs, particularly those taken for the *Gardener's Chronicle*, give an adequate impression of her remarkable colour sense. Her own prose gives it, though only to a person already knowledgeable in flowers, and it can hardly convey her pioneer use of what we now call offbeat colours, such as lime green, or the queer pink of the martagon lily – still referred to as 'dingy' in many garden textbooks, which advocate the garish salmon-and-shrimp hy-brids instead. (The baleful influence of these fish-paste colours on our gardens, starting with the introduction of the *Daily Mail* rose in the 1920s and still going full blast today, was never accepted by Constance with any enthusiasm.)

There are chapters on flowers for occasions, parties, wed-dings, Christmas, restaurants; these were to be expanded in later books, but never repetitively, as Constance's own voy-ages of exploration continued. Over restaurant flowers, she had to admit defeat. When she was called in to suggest an improvement, she always urged one or two bold groups, per-haps on wall vases, as for a party. But restaurant owners remained convinced that their clients would feel neglected without 'the irritating little vase which is just in the way on the small table', and refused to be parted from their two carnations and a bit of fern. 'I think nothing short of an earthquake will bring about reformation here,' she regretfully concludes.

There is a final chapter on vases. The admission that the lovely marble or alabaster tazzas shown in the illustrations were bought 'at very small cost' must have sent the readers of 1934 scurrying to the junk-shops and salerooms. Today's can only envy Constance her luck.

Before the book could appear, two friends had died, Sir William Lawrence, its progenitor, and Norman Wilkinson; Constance pays tribute to them both. And in September, another door closed with the death of George Fletcher. He had retired in 1927, leaving Ireland with general good wishes and an honorary degree from Trinity College, and he and Etty had converted a near-derelict Elizabethan farmhouse in Essex, and made of it a setting for the flair they had passed on to their daughter. He was active to the last, a member of various English educational committees, and chairman of his parish council. His going posed the problem of who was to look after his widow; her meetings with her daughter were as disastrous as ever. It was strangely solved when Heppell Marr volunteered. He had by now retired from India, and Etty had always regarded him as her son, a sentiment no doubt deepened by Constance's rejection of them both. A pleasant house was found for them in Sussex, and the man who had been harsh to wife and daughter proved himself an exemplary son-in-law, devotedly nursing the peevish and fretful old woman to the end.

George Fletcher had lived to see Constance's material success, and with the publication of her first book, to guess at the influence she was to have as an educator, a success which meant much more to him. She had always been loved, and she was by now forgiven. Other pundits of the educational world were not, however, so lenient over what they regarded as her apostasy. Sir Robert Blair ended a generous appreciation of his old friend in *The Times* with the statement that 'Mrs Fletcher, three sons and one daughter survive him. The daughter was a live principal of one of London's compulsory day continuation schools.'

Shav Spry, who was on holiday in France, learnt of his

father-in-law's death through seeing this notice, and in his letter of commiseration to Constance observes mildly: 'I think it is hard for you to be mentioned only as a "live principal".' One of the links that bound them was that they could both see the funny side of a snub.

Both in business and in domestic life, Constance soon felt the need to be on the move again. Burlington Gardens was rapidly becoming outgrown; Colney Park, on the other hand, was too large and costly to run. 'We must find a farm,' Shav Spry pronounced.

The marriage of Prince George, Duke of Kent, to Princess Marina of Greece made 1934 an especially brilliant season, and brought Constance her first royal client. The Duke took the lease of a house in Belgrave Square, almost next door to that of his old friend Lady Portarlington, who gave a fortnightly party at which the young couple met a more varied circle than that of Buckingham Palace. Constance did the flowers for these occasions, and was then invited to do them for the Kents. Of the two, Prince George was the more interested; he was a keen gardener, loved to watch Robbo and Sheila at work, and was amused by their use of bits and pieces from his dinner services. With business booming, more decorators were needed; at the same time, clients inundated Constance with requests to train their daughters. 'It would just suit her, she's so dreamy and artistic,' was frequently offered as a qualification, and Constance would point out, as kindly as she knew how, that it was nothing of the sort. Work with flowers demanded speed, skill, precision; it was nerve-racking, because the material was so perishable; one continually needed to foresee and retrieve disaster. (In the same way, when the flower-club movement started, she would listen wryly to competitors who boasted that it had taken them three hours to compose a piece.)

But there was plainly a need for some form of training, which equally could be used to satisfy the requirements of the shop. The first Constance Spry Flower School was opened in the basement of Sunderland House in Curzon Street, and was an amateurish affair, with only two hours of lectures and demonstrations a day. A good many of the students were debutantes amusing themselves, or girls filling in time before going on to college. But there were always a few with real talent and ambition. They were allowed to help out in the shop as well, and to lend a hand with mossing and wiring on rush orders; then, if they showed sufficient promise, they were given jobs when their course ended.

In this way Constance gathered her staff, and her instinct for finding the right people was seldom mistaken. But in the few instances when it failed her, she was ruthless in dismissal, and rightly so; her success depended on an absolutely maintained standard; only, she could never bring herself to do the dismissing in person. She praised, charmed, encouraged, and kept her team in love with her and with their work, 'a thrilling occupation, continually doing what you really enjoy with a perpetual change of material.' Any disciplinary unpleasantness was deputed to Val Pirie.

Constance was careful to stress to students that they could not expect to become skilled florists in the year of gentle part-time study the course occupied, and that those of them who hoped to have their own businesses would need to employ florists who had gone through the long apprenticeship; but 'a good student can absorb what she needs to execute the simple processes of floristry herself, or to direct others in the carrying out of her designs.' Market procedure and customs, costing, accounts and avoidance of waste were also part of the course, and in those who did start their own shops she always took a maternal interest. There was never anything dog-in-the-manger in her attitude to rivals. When, as occasionally happened, spies from other establishments were sent to sketch the groups in her window, she would laugh and say: 'Never mind, we'll do something different tomorrow.' That students should wish to take the course as part of their general education, as they might have taken one in music or painting, perhaps pleased her best of all. It was proof that she was filling a real educational need. When the Matron of Guy's Hospital told a too-young aspirant to take the flower training and then come back to start her nursing, it seemed to Constance the highest compliment she could receive.

. . . . .

The new shop premises were found at the end of 1934, at 64 South Audley Street, where the firm has been ever since. 'It must be all right because it's farther west,' said Constance anxiously; in many ways she remained naïve, and her notion of a smart London address was that the farther west you went, the smarter it was bound to become. The move, however, could not take place immediately, as a good deal of conversion was necessary, and the shop, bursting at the seams, took over temporary premises in Dover Street.

At the same time, the business was put on a proper footing by being incorporated as a limited liability company, Flower Decorations Ltd., with Constance and Val Pirie as its directors and Eleanor Gielgud as secretary. Shav Spry's name did not appear, but of course he continued to be the principal adviser, and to point out to Constance what she could and could not do. She never quite took no for an answer; she would brood, and presently come up with: 'but couldn't we do it *this* way?' – and in the end, means were generally found. He on his side was very well aware that her flow of ideas, her constant need for new ventures and explorations, were an essential part of her creativeness. If she were thwarted, and forced to fall back on a few well-paying lines, she would dwindle into just another florist, or more probably, grow bored and give up.

In February, two more directors were added to the Board, a chartered accountant colleague of Spry's, and the brilliant young South African dress designer, Victor Stiebel. 'I was there to be on Connie's side', he says, and thereby does himself an injustice; he had proved that a creative artist can also be a successful business man. Not the least of the pleasures success had brought to Constance was that of contact with designers gifted in other fields: with Beverley Nichols and Norah Lindsay as designers of gardens, with Rex Whistler and Oliver Messell as artist decorators. But it was Victor Stiebel who, more than any other new friend, filled Wilkinson's place.

His exquisite clothes were having a success parallel to hers with flowers, and he had recently expanded his house at 22 Bruton Street by taking on a further showroom, decorated by Syrie Maugham, who emphasized its noble Georgian proportions with one of her all-white schemes. It was to be opened with a midnight party. 'You must have Constance Spry to do the flowers,' she told him, 'she's a genius and you'll adore her.' Thereafter, those of us who were privileged to attend Mr Stiebel's twice-yearly collections would always look for the long Spry trail of flowers, usually with lilies among them, on each of the two Adam mantelpieces which fronted each other at the two ends of the great room.

The link between Constance and Victor Stiebel was not clothes, in which he could never really interest her, though she loved fine fabrics, and was delighted to be given the bits left over in the workroom at the end of each season. Her clever fingers turned them into the coloured tablecloths she loved, or into patchwork curtains. He made her a dress or two for her rare evening engagements; one of them, in black velvet, had a small train to give her height. She went upstairs to try it on and came down kicking a flap of velvet in front of her, and saying, 'There's something wrong with this dress of Victor's.' She had put it on back to front.

What delighted him in her was her all-round talent for civilization: for food, furnishings, flowers. She had started something which, it seemed to him, was spreading over the country like a wonderful euphoric disease. He knew from his travels that there was nothing like it on the Continent, nor in America either. He was furnishing a London house, and so became a new comrade in her junk hunts, and they made many discoveries together. Two marble-topped tables were bought for the proverbial song in the Caledonian Market, and a furniture storage place off Tottenham Court Road was another mine. Her own ingenious improvisations were a constant wonder to him. She was making grand-looking 'gesso' tables for her new shop, at no cost at all, by draping half-moons of wood with swags of hessian, the whole thing then being plastered white.

He was fond of Syrie, but knew her for a lion-hunter, with a vulgar streak. Constance, on the other hand, he found without a flaw.

The autumn of 1935 brought Constance the prestige of her first official royal function, the wedding of the Duke of

12. At work on the famous needlework carpet, which soothed her own
and her friends' nerves during the years of war.

13. *Below right:* 'Twentieth century baroque'.

14. *Below left:* Constance Spry watering some of the plants in her conservatory.

Gloucester and Lady Alice Montagu-Douglas-Scott. The Duke of Kent had recommended her work to his brothers, and though she was not yet asked to decorate the Abbey, she had the honour of doing the bride's and bridesmaids' bouquets. The dresses were pale cream, and she used cream flowers with pale brown 'skeletonized' magnolia leaves, then a novelty to English eyes. Today, when the fashion has swung back again to Victorian posies, the group photograph looks over-flowered, yet one can see that it was beautiful, and set a new standard in elegance and grace.

The Prince of Wales at St James's Palace and Fort Belvedere became a regular client, and he, like the Duke of Kent, was a knowledgeable gardener. Robbo remembers the Fort as 'a house that said welcome'. There was a delightful garden of the shrubby, semi-wild type which was coming into fashion, and they were allowed to pick what they liked. There was always a big jigsaw puzzle in the drawing-room, and there was a gramophone to give them music while they worked. She and Sheila took sandwiches, but if Constance accompanied them and the Prince was in residence, she would be invited to lunch with him. He had somehow found out about her work at Homerton, and he would question her closely, and tell her of his own tours in the slum areas, which pressed so heavily on his mind.

Strangely, I have not heard of any other person with whom Constance re-lived the years at Homerton. Possibly His Royal Highness was the only one who took the trouble to ask.

Constance's junk-shop technique applied equally to house-hunting. She was passing through Kent in a taxi on a foggy morning when she saw a derelict fruit-farm looming up out of the fog, and called to the driver to stop. It was exactly the setting Shav Spry had envisaged. Parkgate, Chelsfield, not far from Orpington, is generally agreed to have been the most attractive of Constance's houses and gardens, so that an assessment of her gardening abilities may be undertaken here. 'I was first, and hope to be last, a gardener,' she stated as her creed, but in her second book, *Flowers in House and Garden,* (1937), she qualifies it honestly, 'I had better admit to bias at the outset. I cannot refrain from considering plants primarily for their decorative value when cut.'

She grew, that is to say, largely for cutting; she grew also as a plant collector, always delighted to have some new thing and sure she could squeeze it in somewhere (and as her gardens were on a spacious scale, she always could.) She did not garden as an artist, creating a landscape with plants as Gertrude Jekyll had. If she worked out a scheme, it would be for some corner, rather than for the garden as a whole. Also, until Parkgate, she had been constantly on the move. 'It is always an unhappy experience to be turned out of a garden,' she wrote, but it is an experience the really dedicated gardener takes pains to avoid, whereas she and Spry had shown an almost reckless craving for changes of air. No doubt they believed Parkgate to be a permanency, and certainly they lived there longer than anywhere before, but it was not to be their journey's end.

She made a real effort at landscaping round the charming red brick Georgian farmhouse with its attendant cluster of oasts. 'There had been a good garden there but we had to find it,' Walter Trower recalls. The cobbled yard was turned into a lawn, the fruit-trees thinned, but enough of them left to make a dappled background to a sweep of border, and to form a grove between the lawn and the wild garden. At the far end of this, in a border dug out of the turf and backed by open farmland, were Constance's untidy, tangled, space-consuming darlings, the plants above all others with which her name is associated, the 'old' roses.

The cult of old and species roses was not, of course originated by her; not indeed had it ever been quite lost. Specimens survived as ancient bushes up and down the country, and widely in Irish gardens; her friends the Moores at the Glasnevin Botanic Garden had a collection. So had another noted Irish gardener and designer who now lived and worked in England, Mrs Norah Lindsay. It was seeing the great billowing mounds of these roses in Mrs Lindsay's garden which first gave Constance the idea of forming her own collection; the publication of Edward Bunyard's *Old Garden Roses* in 1936 revealed to her the diversity and scope of the hobby. Thereafter she went ahead with her usual enthusiasm, collecting wherever she travelled, in England and Ireland, in France, in Tunisia, finally on her lecture tours in the United States, where many varieties believed lost had survived in country graveyards. When, towards the end of the war, the old-rose expert Graham Thomas made her acquaintance, he was able to compare her collection with those of other enthusiasts, like Colonel Messel at Nymans or V. Sackville-West at Sissinghurst. Where they had perhaps a dozen each, she had between fifty and sixty.

The disadvantages of old roses, which make them so difficult to accommodate in our present small gardens – their relative brevity of flowering, their untidy habit and vast size of bush – meant nothing to Constance. She had plenty of space, and she never cared about the lasting power of a bloom, either in the garden or in a vase; it was worth growing if it only lasted one night. The words 'labour saving' do not, I think, occur anywhere in her writings. But then, she always disposed of a good deal of labour, both paid and voluntary; 'I never knew anyone so surrounded by little black boys,' an envious acquaintance rather sourly remarked. The favourite picture her friends retain of Constance was her making an entry, on the lecture platform or in her own drawing-room, on some day of high summer, her arms loaded with great fragrant sprays of moss or gallica or centifolia roses, in all their rich colourings of crimson and purple, silvery pink and slaty grey. What one of them has called her 'glorious blowsiness' reached its apotheosis at moments like these.

She would bring back other treasures from her travels, chiefly seeds for the vegetable garden, a splendid affair on the lines of a true French *potager,* and Walter Trower would be asked to grow zucchinis, petits pois, mangetout peas, the real French beans that are picked small as grass, and the tiny cherry tomatoes in sprays, which she chiefly used in vases – though any of his vegetables were liable to suffer this fate, along with fruited branches of cherries or apples from the orchard trees. They were so old, and the fruit not worth much anyway, she would point out when people were shocked.

The garden was rich in matured trees, but she added five trees of the weeping silver lime, *Tilia petiolaris*, buying them in the largest size that could safely move. Sprays cut from these trees, with their extra-large lime-green flowers and silvery leaves, became one of her hallmarks. And in fact two of them did move again, when she left Parkgate, though by that time a firm of specialists with a lorry was needed to transplant them.

Behind the house there were two acres of cutting garden, and two big greenhouses, also devoted to flowers for cutting, and run by a second gardener. This admirable arrangement should have kept Walter's garden inviolate, but of course it did not. Constance would see something in his borders just right for the composition she had in mind, and she would pounce, doing her best to talk him round. In her books he figures – not by name, naturally – as the dragon who must be circumvented, but the gardening reader will sympathize with him, and to those who know him, his modesty and integrity as a person are sufficient answer.

For the most part they got on together very happily, for Constance was never just the mistress giving orders. In the small amount of free time she could command, she shared in the work, finding, as highly-strung people so often do, great comfort in the feel of the earth under her hands. She would come in late and reluctantly, and change her dress in a hurry if friends were expected for dinner, and as like as not, beneath the hem of her evening dress would peep out muddy shoes.

And Walter on his side respected her wide and constantly increasing plant knowledge, her enquiring and inventive mind. He had come to her a raw country boy, and as he says, 'she taught me all I know.'

The move to South Audley Street took place in time to greet the new reign, and for the first time, Constance's staff, now numbering about seventy all told, enjoyed real spaciousness. Three floors provided them with a big, light working basement, an elegant shop, and a special wedding room under the direction of the gifted and versatile Gertrude Gotto. The weddings were unnumerable, and most of them have faded except, perhaps, in the memory of the brides, but one or two stand out because they gave particular satisfaction to Constance herself. There was the Duke of Norfolk's wedding, with bridesmaids in pale blue and the flowers in brilliant clashing reds, undiluted by any note of green. There were weddings in St Paul's, where the vast scale of the building challenged the decorators to produce constructions of branches, hippeastrums, phormium and yucca on an architectural scale in great urns of lead or stone. There was the marriage of Lady Violet Bonham Carter's daughter Laura to Mr Jo Grimond, when St Margarets was decorated entirely with cow-parsley, an exquisitely lacy effect (and requiring an enormous amount of 'conditioning' beforehand.) Similarly, a debutante ball at Claridges Hotel was done with cow-parsley and ox-eye daisies; the management were rather shocked.

And there was the most talked-of nuptial decor of all, designed by Mr Cecil Beaton but carried out by Constance, when his sister Nancy married Sir Hugh Smiley. The bridesmaids were roped together by garlands of flowers, and Constance had the garlands whitewashed, but it had not been foreseen that in the heat of the church the whitewash would flake off, leaving a chalky trail up to the chancel steps and back again. 'It was quite a time,' says George Foss 'before we were allowed into St Margarets again after that.'

Commercially, these immediately pre-war years were Constance's most successful. She published a second book, she wrote innumerable articles on flower arrangement for magazines, and she proved a highly sympathetic broadcaster, being possessed of that rarity, an English lady's voice which gave no effect of condescension. 'She must be coining money,' people started to say. It was never, then or ar any other time, true.

For one thing, she continued to be under-capitalized, so that things had to be done in an expensive way, rent paid out for scattered premises (even after the move to South Audley Street the Flower School still had to be housed across the road). She did not lack for offers of capital, but she had a feminine horror of being, as she put it, in debt, or of giving backers the chance to dictate and interfere. (In the same spirit she refused advances on books from her publishers. 'Suppose I were to die before the book was finished?' she would say.)

And it was also a fact that she was an artist, not a business woman. She liked to have money, but to spend on things that

furthered her art, be it another alabaster vase, or another trip
to collect Tunisian pots at Hammamet, or some piece of old
French furniture that could be turned into a flower table. She
took a childish glee in small shrewdnesses, such as asking a
thousand pounds from a firm of metal-polish manufacturers
who wanted a pamphlet on flower arrangements in metal containers, with text. (They paid up, to her agent's surprise, and
she afterwards expanded the text to form the gay little paper-
back *How to Do the Flowers*; few readers can have noticed that
the majority of the containers are in metal, none of it highly
polished.) But as will be seen, a far more important asset,
which might have made her an international millionaire in the
Helena Rubinstein or Elizabeth Arden class, she threw heed-
lessly away.

With a new Sovereign who honoured her by personal friendship, and with Mrs Ernest Simpson a customer of almost
equally long standing, Constance might well feel that her
prospects were bright. The only cloud on the horizon was a
pending lawsuit. The top floor of the building at South Audley
Street was still let to private residents, and one of them claimed
that by the terms of his lease, business tenants were not to be
permitted above ground-floor level. He brought an action
against the landlord and against Flower Decorations Limited.
The case was not heard till 1938, but Constance worried about
it in the night watches, for she had a feminine terror of the law.

Mrs Simpson was a much-liked client, whose flowers in her
Regent's Park house were usually done by Sheila Young. Like
Syrie Maugham she was fastidious, hated wire-netting to
show, knew nothing about flowers but knew what she liked,
and gave warm praise when it was done. Sheila remembers her
pleasure at spring branches with 'those cute little yellow worms
on'.

All through 1936 her name was increasingly a subject for
gossip, though it was still kept out of the British press. Constance, hotly on the side of true love, summoned the whole
staff and solemnly addressed them. 'These are two of our best
customers, none of you have had anything but kindness from
them, and I want you to be absolutely silent and loyal.' The

promise was given and kept, though when the story broke, re-porters were offering huge bribes to anyone who had the entry at Mrs Simpson's or the Fort.

The Abdication crisis came and passed; the coronation of the new King and Queen, next year, meant greatly increased work for parties and festivities, though Constance had no official commission, nor did she expect one, closely associated as she was with the departed regime. She designed a small crown-shaped table vase, which had a success as a souvenir; it is another item the collector might look out for.

In June came a moving invitation. The Duke of Windsor, at last reunited with the woman for whom he had given up a crown, was to marry her at the Chateau de Candé, the home of her friends the Herman Rogers, not far from Val Pirie's family Franco-Scottish chateau of Varennes. The salon at Candé was to be turned into a chapel for the occasion. Would Constance decorate it?

Constance determined to execute the commission herself, with Val Pirie's assistance. They went first to Paris, where they ordered three dozen Madonna lilies and a quantity of paeonies. Then they hired a car and drove to Varennes. Val's family were away but the gardener and his wife made up beds for them, and for two days they picked like mad – syringa, more paeonies, and great sprays of rambler roses. It would all add up to the sort of decoration Constance loved best – the grandeur of florist's flowers framed in the rich informality of garden picking.

They crammed the car full and made their way to Tours, securing beds not without difficulty, and then drove on to Candé, which was in a state of siege, with reporters from all over the world battering at its gates. Once thankfully inside, they were welcomed with great kindness by Mrs Rogers, and as old friends by Mrs Simpson and the Duke.

The house itself was in a turmoil of preparation, and it was not possible for Constance to do her flowers *sur place*. They were allotted an Orangery at the side of the drive, where they first spread the floor with old copies of *The Times*, found in a chest at Varennes, and then filled buckets and plunged their mountains of flowers for a drink. The scheme was worked out:

two huge pedestals on either side of the improvised altar, flowers for the hall, flowers for the wedding breakfast. In the end, there were vases almost everywhere in the house.

The work took two days, and the Duke, short of occupation as bridegrooms commonly are, joined them to watch it in progress, and to gossip as he had done at the Fort. He was interested by the buckle of Val Pirie's belt, and she knew a momentary confusion; without thinking she had put on a Coronation souvenir. Then he saw the carpets of newspapers, and wanted to know where they came from; when it was explained to him, he began, like any other homesick exile, to read them ancient items of English news from off the floor.

They were presently joined by Cecil Beaton, who was to record the bridal pair (and incidentally the pedestal groups) in his photographs, though as he was not invited to the actual ceremony, he was obliged to take them beforehand. He remembers 'Mrs Spry, robin-like in a picture hat and overalls', and how she and her assistant Miss Pirie, 'two laden Ganymedes, calmly went about their business of decorating the whole chateau with magnificent mountains of mixed flowers.' At midday everyone, household and helpers, sat down together for a snack lunch.

On the wedding morning, they slipped into seats at the back for the short service. The eyes of the world were upon it, but as Val Pirie remembers it, there were only about twenty people actually present, and without the so-English flowers it might even have seemed rather forlorn. They had their share in the simple reception; then the Duke and his bride went south for their honeymoon, and the decorators north-east, back through Blois and Orleans to Paris.

Constance was exhausted. She had not undertaken such hard physical labour since the early days in Belgrave Road, and her feet were so swollen that she could hardly stand. It was late when they reached Paris and found rooms in a hotel, but Val Pirie prevailed on a masseuse to come, and her ministrations were comforting.

Next day, still weary but contented, they returned to London.

<<<<<<<<<<<<<<<<<<<<<<<<<<<<<<<<<<<<<<<

6. CONSTANCE SPRY INC.

Constance's fame had preceded her to the United States, in the form of enthusiastic reports from returning London visitors. In 1937 she was asked to give two lectures on flower arrangement in New York, as part of a fund-raising campaign for the Brooklyn Botanic Garden. Her success was immediate, and led to a nation-wide lecture tour under the auspices of the Garden Clubs of America; they attracted larger audiences than the clubs had ever known before.

She did not, then or at any time, demonstrate flower arrangement, though she might do a group beforehand to stand on the platform table. The technique of doing a group 'from behind' had yet to be evolved, and when it was, Constance always had someone to do it for her. She spoke to her slides, and with this her audience was perfectly satisfied. Her friendliness, her attractive voice, and the complete absence of that condescension which sometimes afflicts the English lecturer when confronted by American listeners, won all hearts.

The love affair was mutual. She was enchanted to find that she might range as widely as she pleased, speaking on gardening, or on house decoration, and expressing all her theories about the beauty which ordinary people could create for themselves.

She also had much to learn. She found that the Americans were not, like the English, a nation of gardeners. There was no tradition of cottage gardening, spilling over into suburban plots. The 'yard' round the house might contain flowering shrubs and trees, but it would be most unlikely to have a cutting border. There were, of course, large and famous gardens, which she was taken to see, and where she found herself greatly excited by new material. But they were invariably the property of the really rich, and were usually worked by immigrant staffs, from Europe or from Japan.

The Garden Clubs did not at all correspond to the English village horticultural society. They were an entirely feminine movement, the largest in America, and were primarily social, not horticultural. They did much excellent work, in the preservation of landscape, the beautification of cities, the conservation of old houses and so forth, and some of their members owned gardens, but very few actually got down to work with spade and hoe. The possession of a large drawing-room where fund-raising meetings could be held was a better qualification for membership than green fingers.

As a part of their activities the clubs held flower shows, which were in fact flower-arrangement shows, something still unknown in England, where the arrangement class was no more than an adjunct of the horticultural show, and might well be a few jamjars stuck away in a corner of the marquee. Constance was hugely impressed by the preparations for a big American show, the alcoves, niches and shadow-boxes, the dining-tables, mantelpieces and other bits of furniture used to reconstruct corners of rooms, the elaborate lighting. It opened up new possibilities, which the Americans themselves, she felt, had not yet fully explored.

For there was a good deal about the actual arrangement which disquieted her. Its material was bought rather than grown, and was therefore prone to flout her basic rule of studying the growing plant, and at the same time it was bedevilled by what seemed to her a great many arbitrary rules. Wild material might not be combined with garden, nor greenhouse with outdoor, thereby cutting across the Spry principle of blending purely for aesthetic effect. And the intense competitiveness of the American show worried her; the same element would later worry her in the English counterpart.

The most pervasive influence on American flower arrangement was Japanese, a vogue which had started, naturally enough, in California, and spread eastwards. Constance was always careful to pay lip-service to the charm of Oriental styles, and indeed, when asked on several occasions to decorate at the Japanese Embassy in London, had displayed an unwonted diffidence and been very willing to adapt her work. (Further adaptations of it, very attractive to Western eyes, have been made by Sheila Macqueen and others of her following since her death.) But temperamentally she was not attuned to its austerities; her instinct was always for the billowing and the lavish.

That it suited the American pocket was obvious. Flowers were costly, and the American florist was willing to sell an assorted 'Ikebana' bunch. But did it, she wondered, suit the average American interior? 'Am I wrong, or is there a frequent and insistent oriental influence shown in the flower arrangements of American women who would not think of furnishing their rooms in Japanese furniture or dressing exclusively in kimonos?'

What she too often seemed to see when she looked into the illuminated niches was something over-precious and stylized. the product of anxious study rather than of free self-expression. 'While I admire this very highly specialized art,' she wrote on her return, 'and like delicate arrangements, and precise arrangements, and beautiful line and good gradations of colour, every now and then I lose patience and want to sweep everything finicking aside and drag in boughs of apple blossom, or masses of shouting colours, bring the outside in somehow.'*

To 'bring the outside in somehow' might well be her mission to America: to break down the inhibitions, to get more people growing and gardening, and bringing in material from the woods and hedgerows – 'garbage from the golf course,' one of them called it. To this day, it is remarkable how little interest Americans take in the rich variety of wild flowers to be found in their woods.

The eager response to her lectures, the close questioning, encouraged her to believe that the moment was propitious. She received much hospitality on her tours, and stayed in houses to which her ideas had already penetrated, and in others which were flowerless because the hostess told her, 'I was nervous to

---

* *A Garden Notebook*, pp 158–9.

arrange anything for such an expert as yourself.' There seemed to be a public waiting, as there had been in England; but perhaps, like so many visiting Englishwomen, she was too easily impressed by the similarities of the cousinhood, and did not take the profound differences made by history and climate sufficiently into account.

As well as lecturing, she appeared on radio and television networks, and arranged for American publication of her next book, but there was no question of her embarking on an American business venture; she had quite enough worries with the London one. And then it was handed to her on a plate. A group of New York friends who had admired her work, all of them wealthy society hostesses and several of them garden-owners, offered to give her a shop.

The offer was entirely disinterested. The leaders of the group were Mrs James V. Forrestal whose husband was Secretary of the Navy, and Mrs Ogden Mills, whose husband was Secretary of the Treasury. To none of the ladies did a return on their capital greatly matter; their object was to give Constance scope to revolutionize the American house and garden, and a New York business was envisaged as the fountain whence her influence would flow. She was to receive a small number of shares and a generous percentage of the profits. In return she would give her name, lend some of her staff to train the American one, and be present personally for the five months of the winter season, returning to London for the summer.

Constance was overwhelmed. She ecstatically accepted it all – though one can't help wondering how, once the first flush of enthusiasm was over, she would really have endured separation from Shav Spry and her garden for five months every year.

Her London fellow-directors, though they had their hands full with the lawsuit over the Audley Street premises, did sound a note of caution, which was strongly echoed by Spry. Her name, he suggested, was potentially an asset at least as valuable as the capital the ladies were to put up; it should be safe-guarded. For once in a way, she would not listen to him. She was dazzled by the generosity of her friends' offer, and the out-right gift of her name was the least, she said, that she could bring to the concern. Spry had made it a rule not to interfere when he saw that her mind was made up, and he said no more.

Constance poured out her enthusiasm and impatience in letters to Mrs Mills, and certainly no time was being lost on either side of the Atlantic. A manager for the new venture was found in Patricia Easterbrook, a dynamic young Australian who had run her own flower shop, and had made a coast-to-coast tour of the States, studying its floristry. She spent the summer learning all the work at South Audley Street, and then accompanied Val Pirie to Czechoslovakia to buy huge quantities of 'Christmas nonsense', since the American shop was to have a winter opening. A decorator and a florist were asked to go out for six months and train their American opposite numbers, and there was no lack of volunteers. Sheila Macqueen recalls her chagrin that she was considered too young.

Constance's choice fell on Margaret Watson as the decorator; she was second in experience only to Robbo, and had had the same training, first at Studley and then under Mrs Ashley's eagle eye at Broadlands. She was a fair, graceful, very English-looking young woman in her early thirties. The florist was a little dark Cockney, Ivy Pierotti, 'Pierrot' to everyone, who had magical fingers though she appeared to have no ideas in her head.

The American ladies formed their incorporated company, with Mrs Forrestal as President, and bought a private house at 62 East 54th Street. To help them with its conversion to shop and showroom, Mrs Forrestal approached her friend Mrs Robert Lovett, a woman who, had it been necessary for her to earn her own living, might well have been the American Constance Spry. Adele Lovett had not at this time heard of Constance or her ideas, but she and her husband owned a 24-acre estate on Long Island, with a huge, partly wild garden that was a passion with both of them, and for years she had been making towering pillar and pedestal arrangements with a Flemish inspiration, to suit her high-ceilinged rooms, and using in them material from flower and shrub borders, vegetable garden, field or orchard, with a truly Spry-like lavishness of line and disregard of convention and rule.

I am indebted to Mrs Lovett's own recollections of that excited summer:

'Early in the summer of 1938, Josephine Forrestal came to see me. She told me that she and several other women had arranged to bring Constance Spry over to this country to open a shop in New York, similar to her London shop, which they would back. Josephine asked me to help them plan the shop and act as one of the decorators; she said the reason why she wanted me to do this was that I was the only person in America whose approach to flower arrangements was the same as Mrs Spry's. She also thought I could be very helpful to Constance on account of my special knowledge of American horticulture. The backers had bought a private house at 62 East 54th Street and we were to make it over into a flower shop, decorate it and have it ready for Mrs Spry's arrival in late summer.

'I accepted with enthusiasm and we got to work at once. I suggested to Josephine that I work without pay until at least the first of the year, as an apprentice. The plan was for Mrs Spry to be in New York from the first of October to the first of June, managing the shop during the New York season, and returning to the London shop for the London season from June to October.

'Harold Sterner, the architect, (he had built the Forrestal house at Beekman Place and our house on the East River) was to remake 62 East 54th Street into a shop for us. We set to work at once on the structural alterations, and by the time Constance arrived the shop was nearly ready. The show-room for fresh flowers with its ice-boxes was on the ground floor front, the fresh flower work-room and storage ice boxes at the back. The second floor was all showrooms, furnished rather barely and elegantly, like parlours. There were more work-rooms on the third floor for making the potpourri, painting and waxing flowers for her artificial arrangements, and making up the Christmas glitter, wreaths, sprigs and kissing boughs.

'Soon after Constance's arrival she came to Pending, our country place at Locust Valley, and I was charmed at once. She was a small round cheerful person with enormous vitality, a delicious sense of humour, warmth, and exquisite manners. She was, besides, incredibly capable, imaginative, practical and talented. We had a big picking garden at Pending, a vegetable garden surrounded by four long wide herb borders, and an orchard behind it with peach, apple and pear trees; a big field full of grasses and wild flowers; and masses of flowering and berried shrubs, and flowering and fruiting trees, from all of which I picked for my own enormous arrangements.

'Constance was interested to find material here that was not available in England, and I took her everywhere I thought there might be something new for her to see and use.'

Constance approved the building, with its pretty ground-floor bow window to give an English touch, and supervised the interior decoration, which needless to say was white. Margaret Watson and Pierrot, arriving early in September, found her installed in a hotel near the shop, and employing every spare moment in the devising of more 'nonsense'. As soon as the walls were dry, they got down to the teaching of the American recruits, and the piling up of stocks for the opening.

Adele Lovett takes up the account:

'She taught us to make all the things she needed, potpourri, pomander balls, Christmas ornaments glittered with gold or silver. She showed us how to mount the skeletonized magnolia leaves which came in packages of single leaves from the wholesalers; these were wired on to twigs and branches to make lovely frail sand-coloured boughs, to mix with her dried flower arrangements, or to use instead of fresh greens in her flower bouquets. We learned to paint and wax and wire the artificial paper flowers that were her specialty, and to make her giant fresh cabbage roses and enormous carnations, that became the rage for corsages.' These, it appears, were 'cannibalized" from a dozen flowers wired together, and would seem to have been Constance's one lapse from taste; it is sad to learn that they were so successful.

'We had a store-room full before the shop opened. Constance had also brought over some moulds of her specially designed vases, and we found a place in Brooklyn that could duplicate them for the shop. There were half a dozen shapes, all finished inside with a high gloss, and outside with a matt finish so that they could be tinted to suit the room in which they were to be used – a new idea here and one that was very popular.

'Constance insisted that all of us wear the same uniform in the shop, herself included – an unbleached muslin coat with a widely flaring skirt and wide sleeves, designed by Claire McCardle, who was then one of the leading New York dress designers. They could be slipped on over our street dresses, and were very practical and smart. The shop routine was to have a morning break, 'Elevenses', a cup of tea and a bun, and another about 3 p.m. Constance was always there, full of the latest news and developments, and making it all amusing with her delicious sense of humour – we all adored her.

'Long before the opening, the shop was a popular meeting place for some of the smartest people in town: the backers, bringing future customers; decorators; the press; or just people going through town who had known Constance in Europe and wanted to say hello. I remember New York had its first hurricane that autumn. All day long the house shook with the wild wind, and people came in sodden from the streets for shelter. Constance made us take away their wet clothes, and wrap them in our work coats, while we dried their clothes on the radiators and gave them hot tea. It was like a party all day. It wasn't until I drove myself home to Long Island after work that evening that I realized what a milling storm it had been, with the great trees down across the roads and the cars pinned under them, flooded fields, debris and breakage everywhere.'

The shop started business on 4 November, but the grand opening was a cocktail party at eleven the night before, when most of smart New York turned up, parking was solid all along 54th Street, and the street musicians did a roaring trade. The bow-window framed a single big group, exquisitely lighted, and the shop inside was a glittering sight, people sitting all up the beautiful staircase and round the gallery looking down on the animated scene. The staff displayed their muslin coats and all had upswept hairdos, an idea novel in a New York still devoted to the long bob.

The press were appreciative next morning. The *New York Herald* found that 'when Nature doesn't produce just what she wants, Mrs Spry doesn't hesitate to create something of her

≪≪≪

15. Constance Spry choosing a position for one of her flower prints.

>>>

16 and 17. H. E. 'Shav' Spry and Constance at Ard Daraich, the holiday house they rented in Scotland – photographs taken by their American friend Helen Robbins Milbank, a few months before Constance's seventieth birthday.

own – two little trees, for instance, which stand at the entrance of the shop, made of brilliant bay leaves wired on in symmetrical rows, leaves that she brought back from Europe 'by the yard'. Of special interest are her winter flowers and vases of dried leaves, and magnolia leaves that have been turned into shadows by a special treatment. Milkweed pods are used in contrast with strange dried lotus and enormous pine cones in other arrangements. The new shop also contains a room for brides decorated in the mood of romance . . .'

And another reporter declared that 'no one, we venture to say, will pass the shop without a prolonged pause. Within, there is much to challenge the visitor's interest – and practically nothing that suggests the traditional American flower shop.'

Thus launched, and with the Social Register as backing, the shop could hardly fail, and Constance was able to go home for Christmas knowing that her staff faced a pressure of work that was overwhelming. It does not seem to have occurred to her that she was repeating the mistake of Belgrave Road, that to start in a small way and a side street in New York made even less sense in 1938 than it had done in London in 1928, and that two decorators and a florist were being asked to do what was done in London by some twenty. If she did not contribute capital to the venture, she should at least have contributed a dozen trained staff.

Patricia Easterbrook was obliged to drive her little team hard, and to undertake a great deal of decorating herself, as well as the management of the business side. (She showed much of Val Pirie's energy and adaptability, and has since, under her married name of Patricia Roberts, achieved fame as a decorator in her own right.) And Adele Lovett learnt what it meant to be one of Constance's 'black boys'. 'There was no such thing as a normal working day in the plant business. Funerals, big parties, weddings – whatever the reason, you started as early as necessary, and worked late until the job was done.'

Superb examples of the Spry manner were achieved and are remembered: all-white coming-out parties, or cream-and-gold ones with the skeletonized leaves well in evidence; a party on the St Regis Roof for which the host wanted pink lilies when only white could be found, and the whites had their faces done with pink theatrical face powder, and no one realized ... The numbers of people who found they could afford, even at New York prices, to have fresh flowers done regularly in their houses increased month by month. The windows of leading stores held Spry arrangements, Bergdorf Goodman in particular proving almost as valuable an advertisement as Atkinsons had been. Store flowers had to be done on a Sunday, which meant that somebody worked a seven-day week. Sometimes, it seemed to them that they worked a twenty-four hour day as well.

By the time Constance returned, the two English girls had had enough. Their six months were up, and Ivy Pierotti, who was engaged, made it clear that she was going home to be married. But Margaret Watson was persuaded to stay on for the summer, and to undertake the shop's most important commission yet, the flowers for the British Pavilion at the New York World's Fair.

Great vases of boughs and leaves on the ground floor asserted Constance's love of the all-green group, and on the first floor a semi-circular display of heraldry had niches at either side for two more huge vases – ladders were needed to do them – which picked up the heraldic colours, scarlet and blue and gold; it was almost a foretaste of Constance's scheme for the next Coronation. She stayed on for the opening, and for the visit of King George VI and Queen Elizabeth, then went back to London. Margaret Watson was left to tend the vases and battle against increasing ill-health and overstrain. Finally, she collapsed with thyroid trouble, and in the autumn had to be invalided home.

There was now no resident English representative of the Spry style, and Constance's promised return in October, with a whole new collection of leaves and baubles and notions from Czechoslovakia, was anxiously looked for by the ladies on the board. But Constance did not return in October. Instead, England and Germany went to war, and the Czechs found themselves occupied in quite another way.

One result of the outbreak of war was a recession in the luxury trades; a temporary recession – it would take Pearl

Harbor to bring real austerity into American homes – but of course the board of Constance Spry Inc. were not to realize this. Another was that Constance's two staunchest supporters, Mrs Forrestal and Mrs Mills, had their energies deflected back into their husbands' political careers. The same thing happened to Mrs Lovett; her banker husband was appointed assistant secretary to the Secretary of War – he later became Secretary of Defence himself – and she departed to Washington, whence she did not return till 1954.

The remaining backers grouped themselves under Mrs William Thayer, who had a wider experience of business methods than any of them, and their appeals to Constance to keep her promise and inject more of her vitality into the flagging concern grew more and more frantic. Constance's replies make tragi-comical reading. She can't come because it would be dishonourable to leave England in her hour of need, then because of worry over the results of the London lawsuit, then because there are royal and other prestige events that she can't possibly drop. As for the American customers who are complaining that they no longer see Mrs Spry, that is unreasonable; it has never been practicable for her to see clients individually. But next month perhaps, or next year, she may see her way clear to come.

What actually happened was that it was a very unwilling Margaret Watson who returned. . . .

Margaret Watson had been turned down for war work on account of her health record, and Constance had most earnestly striven to convince her that helping to keep the New York business going was an equally valuable contribution to the war effort, and to the maintenance of British prestige. She received a warm welcome, and many of her clients came back to the shop, even if their spending was no longer so lavish. But of course she could not be a substitute for Constance, nor could she tell the Board straight out, in reply to their persistent questioning, that she did not think Constance would ever face the ordeal of an Atlantic crossing in war-time. (And it *was* an ordeal, one before which many young men of fighting age had been known to flinch.) It was only a matter of time, of course, before the ladies grasped the position for themselves.

And so, when another New York florist approached them and offered to take over the business, name and all, on advantageous terms, they accepted. It is hard to blame them. They had not gone into it for profit, but equally, being amateurs, they had not envisaged an actual loss. Constance had not kept her side of the bargain, and there was no guarantee that she would ever do so. She had brought not only prosperity, but fun and glamour, and it was largely for the fun and glamour that they had backed her. Without her there was nothing but grind and worry, which they were not prepared to undertake.

The new management moved the shop from its charming but tucked-away premises on to Fifth Avenue, where nobody could miss it, and restyled it on the lines of the conventional American flower shop. It concentrated on the line it realized to be the most paying, Constance's 'arts' – for an American home will accept high-class artificial flowers where a corresponding English one will not. It was one of the first flower businesses to use the new material, plastic, and its continued success has proved the acumen with which it has gauged its markets.

Constance at first attempted to do a little back-seat driving. She urged an all-white decor, she badgered the unfortunate Margaret Watson with suggestions. But Miss Watson soon realized that the Spry style was no longer wanted. Her arrangements were altered or dispensed with; the beautiful vases brought out from Europe for the shop's use, or found in junk shops on Third Avenue, were sold to customers. Soon she too resigned.

It is doubtful if Constance ever fully grasped the implications of what she had brought on herself and her successors – though Spry would have been more than human if he had not endeavoured to make it clear. It meant that a firm bearing her name were now at liberty to market throughout the United States goods bearing her famous and distinctive signature, over the design of which she had not a vestige of control.

She did acknowledge defeat to the extent of allowing the London business to be renamed. It was still Flower Decorations, but with a rival Constance Spry Inc. across the Atlantic, it seemed sensible to alter its title to Constance Spry Limited, which was done in March , 1940. But the existence of two disparate Constance Spry firms continued to puzzle the public.

To an American correspondent who wrote for enlightenment, some time after the war, Constance replied that the New York shop had nothing to do with her, it had been started by some friends in her honour and merely called after her. True as far as it went, but a trifle disingenuous, and the enquirer must have felt himself as baffled as before.

It is undeniable that Constance's American venture had had bad luck. A small new luxury business was bound to be shaken, and very likely killed, by the outbreak of a world war. All the same, one is bound to ask whether, even if it had succeeded, it could ever have been more than a small luxury business? Could Constance's dream, of a whole continent gardening and flower-arranging in her manner, have come true?

Has it, for that matter, come true anywhere except in Great Britain?

The answer seems to be that it hasn't, because it is essentially suited to a garden-owning populace in a mild climate. Otherwise, it comes too expensive. Constance maintained that 'flowers are for everyone', but they can only be for everyone where they are easily and pretty well universally grown.

Not only is gardening a struggle against a hostile climate over large sections of North America (and the late arrival of the New England spring must be a recurrent heartbreak) but the increasingly peripatetic way of life of the middle classes is against it. It is no uncommon thing for a family to move on to another house every two years. But it takes from four to ten years for gardens to produce fine pickable material of any size.

Further, Americans need, or like, to keep their interiors at a high temperature, which means that cut flowers have a short life. House-plants are more practical. Even a woman wealthy in her own right, like Mrs Lyndon B. Johnson, has recorded that one of the things she missed most when her husband left the White House was no longer having fresh flowers in the room every day.

This preference for hot rooms may also explain why our

continental neighbours don't practise flower arranging as Constance had evolved it. Even the Dutch and the Belgians, from whom she may be said to have derived her style, feel happier with house-plants, and the average French florist sells nothing else. Of course house-plants can be, and increasingly are, 'arranged' in groups too, but they can never lend themselves to the fluidity of cut material.

This is not to say that the beauty created by Constance was not appreciated. It was, and it still is; it remains an ideal even for people who have no intention of trying to emulate it. Her American lectures drew enthusiastic audiences, and so do the lecture-demonstrations of present-day visitors like Sheila Macqueen. (But Mrs Macqueen herself believes that she seldom leaves converts behind her.) On the Continent, English flower arrangers carry all before them in the big international festivals like the Ghent Floralies or Monte Carlo. An English church, cathedral or other public building decorated for a flower festival is a sight our foreign visitors increasingly ask to see. The danger now is that through economic pressure and over-population, we English will be driven out of our private gardens. The world will be the poorer if we are.

In spite of the short time she actually spent in the States, Constance's impact was a real one, and she is still, to a surprising extent, personally remembered; as Patricia Easterbrook puts it:

'Flowers are flowers, and she opened their eyes to the beauty of form – whether it was a poppy, a seed pod, a bunch of grass or a lovely leaf. She talked with great horticultural knowledge, which they respected, and she arranged with such joy and abandon that she released them from the Garden Club panic pressure and the Ikebana stuff. Not the whole country – it was too big a job for a couple of trips – but her name is still known after all these years, and it's not because of the hats she wore'

7. BACK TO SCHOOL

In giving her worries over the South Audley Street lawsuit as a reason for not returning to America, Constance was sincere enough. It threw her into a fever of anxiety. She was far too nervous to go into the witness-box, so Val Pirie represented the firm, was cross-examined for two hours, and was complimented by the Judge on the way she had given her evidence. Lady Violet Bonham Carter, as a distinguished customer, also spoke for them, and confirmed that the business was a quietly conducted one, which could not possibly incommode tenants on the top floor.

But the terms of the complainant's lease were specific, and the case was given against the landlord and Flower Decorations. They were ordered to confine themselves to the basement and the ground floor.

What had seemed a minor disaster was, ironically, righted by a major one, the outbreak of war, which would in any case have rendered the original premises far too large. To Constance, 'my third war' seemed at first the ruin of everything dear. (In fact it was her fourth war, but she says herself that the Boer War had not impinged much on her young life.) When next she visited Swanley Horticultural College, her friend Dr Kate Barratt found her near despair. Would flowers, and beauty, and all she had worked for, ever be wanted again? Dr Barratt replied robustly that of course they would, just as gardening would. She planned to carry on, and she urged Constance to do the same. Constance returned to London much heartened. 'Come what may I shall keep this business going and your jobs open,' she told the staff.

The men melted away overnight; the girls trickled off more gradually, into war jobs or marriage. And for a time the shop ran a real risk of having to close; then people grew tired of the 'phoney war' and started to buy flowers again. Presently the small remaining staff found themselves almost busy, for Covent Garden carried on its flower section, the embassies and other prestige customers kept up a decorative front, the war weddings and funerals needed flowers on a modest scale.

Down at Chelsfield, Constance flung herself into food production, jamming and preserving everything that could be preserved, enlarging the vegetable garden, arranging to keep hens, buying a horse and cart to replace the car. Vegetables were sold alongside flowers in the shop. An ARP team was formed, with Constance, in a uniform several sizes too large for her, as its willing but incompetent tail. They practised extinguishing smoke-bombs in a shed, and Constance, for all her anxious determination, managed to wreck the team by reducing the others to hysterical laughter.

When the war began in earnest, Parkgate found itself directly on the path of the German bombers, and the balloon barrage went up all around it. Constance did her round of nightly duty as a warden, all the more creditably because she was terrified, and covering up her terror with jokes about her comical appearance. The train service to London was erratic, but somehow she always got through to the shop. And it too was spared, though the glass was shattered several times. She has recorded how, 'after one particularly unpleasant night, when the floor of the shop was deep in water from the firemen's hoses and the whole place was in a dim half-light because of the broken and boarded-up windows, a customer came in early for flowers, and because of the friendliness which was one of the features of those times everyone gathered round to talk. As she left we thanked her and apologized for so much confusion; she gave an indifferent glance at the mess around her and a smiling one at the flowers she carried, and remarked that in her view flowers made one feel normal.'

This, as Constance came to see it, was her function in the war, to make people feel normal, and to hold out the hope of better times. Invitations came in for her to lecture to the women in uniform; she accepted gladly, fighting her way about the country in the crowded trains and making too her weekly visit to Swanley, now evacuated to the Midlands. She learnt much from these tours. She was in contact with people of all classes, as she had not been since the days of Homerton, and found from questions after the lectures that she must dispel an impression given unconsciously by her books, that her style was strange and esoteric, or else only for the rich.

A letter written to her in the last year of her life, by someone who had heard her lecture at the time of Dunkirk, sums up what many in her audiences must have felt. 'You wore navy, a white frilly jabot, a bracelet of dangling seals, you brought to all of us a sense that "the world will still go on", in spite of the news from Belgium, particularly bad at that time. I was engaged to a gunner officer, posted missing, though he turned up next month from Dunkirk ... You spoke of old roses in old gardens and held us spellbound, and at the end thanked us for listening to you on what seemed a trivial and unimportant matter at this grim time in our history. So, nineteen years and three sons later, we have our own roses, and I would like you to know how long your words stayed with me.'

Her genius for improvising a decoration was stimulated by the steadily increasing scarcity of anything to do it with. Victor Stiebel, who had closed his business and joined the Army, was stationed at a Stately Home in mid-Wales. The officers' mess wished to return local hospitality by giving a ball, but the place was semi-derelict, its panelling boarded up, bits of army furniture standing about forlornly in its great rooms. Constance was summoned and came down, took the measurements of the horrible furniture, dyed yards of hessian in bright colours and got covers made. She sent down flowers from London, cajoled the remaining gardener into giving her background material, did enormous wall groups, and cajoled the Sappers into lighting them. Everyone put on their best clothes, and the ball was an occasion of splendour, quite in the tradition of the Duchess of Richmond's, (equally held in improvised premises), before Waterloo.

Constance's solace on these frequent and often hellishly uncomfortable journeys was working at her floral carpet. It had been begun on her American lecture tours, and was being worked in petit-point, though she had never done tapestry stitching before. She got twenty-four old flower and fruit pictures reproduced on canvas and set to work; then 'I began to think I had started too late in life and would never do twenty-four squares this side of the grave, and to wonder whether I should adapt my first square to an outsize pincushion.' Her remedy was the usual one; friends were set to work, carrying their squares about in their gas-mask cases. By the end of the war the carpet was finished, and was laid on the drawing-room floor of her last house, Winkfield, where it got very hard wear and eventually wore out. A pity; it should have been treated as an heirloom and hung on a wall; but saving things and keeping them for 'best' was never Constance's way.

Nor was this her only experiment in textile design. Even in the darkest days, the Government saw the need to keep design going with a view to regaining exports after the war. Bettie Smail, daughter of one of George Fletcher's colleagues, was then designer for a Lancashire cotton firm, and asked that Constance should be called in to inspire her. Miss Smail would go down to Parkgate, and they would go round the garden together, Constance selecting and assembling posies and colour combinations for her visitor to paint. The air-raid siren often sounded, and they might take shelter under the stairs; usually they were too absorbed to notice. At the end of the session, Constance would go into the kitchen and assemble a delicious cheese and salad meal.

Everyone remembers Parkgate in the war years as a haven of beauty, comfort and good food. It was always full to bursting, with Marjorie Russell and Flo Standfast as more or less permanent residents and others of the circle arriving on leave, though how Constance fitted them into a house which basically had five bedrooms was a mystery. Also, how she fed them so well; for she vehemently denied using the black market. American friends sent parcels, and there must surely have been country sources of supply, but chiefly it was through the trouble she herself took in cooking the vegetables produced by the garden, and her brilliant use of salads and herbs.

A regular visitor of those days was Helen Kirkpatrick, who

had come over as an American war correspondent, with an introduction from Constance's lecture agent in New York. Previous visits had given her the impression, general among her countrymen, that England is a good country to look at but not a good one to feed in, and naturally, war-time stringency had not improved the menus. At Parkgate it was otherwise. Although never before interested in either cooking or gardening, Miss Kirkpatrick loved to watch Constance at work, and she stresses, as so many have done, that uncanny faculty for teaching and arousing interest without appearing to do so:

'Her methods – if they could be called conscious methods – were subtle. She never lectured; she listened, and somehow the questions she put seemed suddenly to bring things into focus and to give them a different perspective. I say this because Connie was in many ways a foster-mother to me, and I confided in her anything and everything, and asked her advice. I can't remember her offering an opinion, but in the end I had an idea of what she thought. Her subtlety and finesse were such that one sensed, rather than heard, her judgments.

'When I moved into a mews house, Connie planned the window boxes. Some were flowers but two had herbs. I knew less than nothing about cooking and herbs were totally foreign to me. She didn't tell me what she was doing or what was there, but waited for me to come and ask. Perhaps she assumed that I knew – though she was well aware of my ignorance – but I do think her method of teaching was to allow one to discover and to inquire.'

One of the pleasures Helen Kirkpatrick enjoyed during 1941 was to sit at Constance's kitchen table and read through the latest additions to the book in progress (for which she was later to write a gay and spirited foreword). For Constance had decided that a further contribution she could usefully make to the war effort was a cookery book, adapted, as her own cooking was, to the exigences of the time. The title chosen for it was a brilliant inspiration of Shav Spry's: *Come Into the Garden, Cook.*

Constance writes as an amateur cook, and indeed, is nervous lest she may have infringed copyrights, for her recipes are

taken from here, there and everywhere, from family scrap-
books (many from Val Pirie's French family), from her travels
in America, France and Tunis, from her friend Rosemary
Hume's book *Au Petit Cordon Bleu*. Adapting them to a kitchen
at war is her share of the work, and it chiefly involves taking a
great deal more trouble than the average Englishwoman was
prepared to go to. For this she does not apologize; if the
French cooks can bother, she tells us, so can we. (She was not
to foresee that Frenchwomen, too, would bother less as time
went on.) She is indignant at the idea that rationing is something to complain about; thinking of her dear hosts the Hensons near the starvation line in Tunisia, she reminds us how
well-off we are compared to those in enemy-occupied countries.
But she is careful not to scold. The cookery she proposes is to
be gay and elegant, not what the Irish call 'famine food'. It
must look appetising, but not at the expense of taste. 'I sometimes feel that accent is more on trimmings than on fundamen-
tal preparation,' she says. (That this was true in the darkest
days of war, I can confirm. I was one of a press party on a
visit to an Army cookery school, and we found the head
instructor demonstrating how to make canapés look like little
boats.)

The garden, visible through the kitchen door in Lesley
Blanch's comical and charming illustrations, is the sort of exquisitely ordered French *potager* Constance adored. There are
suggestions for uncommon vegetables one might grow in it,
and new ways of dealing with the more usual ones. For those
who have no garden there is the possibility of a herb box like
those she made for Helen Kirkpatrick, or even just a herb
flowerpot on the windowsill.

The little book had a warm welcome and a steady sale,
not just to the end of war or to the end of rationing, which
lasted much longer; it is in fact selling today. Constance herself, in the introduction she wrote for its 1952 edition, felt that
elements in it had dated . . . but I wonder. We do not live in
a world of plenty, though luxury cookbooks that pullulate
nowadays might make one believe otherwise. There have always been people thankful to have margarine to cook with,
and soon, there may be a great many more.

But the importance of the book to Constance's biographer is that it so clearly shows her mind returning to what had always been its true bent, that of an educator. She is driven to brood, as indeed most of us were, on the enormous changes war has brought about, on the likelihood that many of them will be permanent, on the snobbery and extravagance of the past which will be better abandoned, but on the other hand, on its cultural traditions which it would be a thousand pities to let die. She is aware that a generation is growing up without any knowledge of *les douceurs de la vie*. She thinks of Homerton, where children came from homes without culture, yet were so quickly receptive to anything she could provide in the way of creativeness and beauty. She wants to have a 'continuation school' again.

She also foresees the breakdown of domestic service, so that the key to gracious living will be the catch-phrase the new generation will invent: 'Do it yourself'. She ponders the bridging of that gulf, so much resented in her own girlhood, between the academically clever girls and the domesticated duffers. The highbrow cook of the 1960s is already on the way.

The whole philosophy underlying her school of the future is expressed in the opening Argument of this unpretentious little book; and although she is writing primarily for the daughters of the well-to-do, and it was for them that she was to found her school, she yet foresaw that for some of them, a creative approach to the domestic arts might be more than just a source of satisfaction. It might also be a livelihood, giving them 'a talisman in times of stress, and a reassuring sense of independence and power.'

The obvious time to start educational ventures would be the ending of the war, when young people would come out of the Forces and need retraining for civilian life; and as the war news grew less gloomy, so Constance's auspices looked good. The shop was already surprisingly prosperous. One result of Pearl Harbor had been to turn Grosvenor Square into a Little America, and officers and GIs alike had the pleasant habit of 'bunching' their girls in South Audley Street, just around the corner.

There was every sign that the staff would be regained. The florists and the 'arts' girls, with their deft fingers, made admirable munitions workers, but in spite of their long hours, some of those on night shift would come back to the shop by day, to keep their hands in at the work they loved. Several of the decorators were now married women with young children, like Sheila Macqueen, and being exempt from war work, they were able to come in part-time. Covent Garden's meagre supply of flowers was supplemented by a regular flow from private gardens, often made up into mixed bunches and nosegays by the garden owners; it is a pity that this excellent idea is not encouraged by the floristry trade today. The shop had a shelter in the basement, but once the shock of the first raids was over, the staff seldom bothered to use it by day.

And Constance was gaining an invaluable ally in Rosemary Hume. They had known each other for years. Rosemary had been a schoolfellow of Val Pirie's, and she was one of the first Englishwomen to take the Cordon Bleu course in Paris (though she says that in those days it merely involved attending lectures, and that she learnt her practical cooking in her mother's kitchen), and one of the first to work as a freelance chef. She cooked for parties in private houses, and would if requested give lessons to the resident cook, sometimes provoking resentment and getting saucepans thrown at her head.

She had cooked for Constance's parties from the days of the Abinger rectory onwards, and gave occasional lessons to Gladys Trower, Walter's wife, who was now cook at Parkgate. Later she had her own restaurant and cookery school in Sloane Street. Constance had an enormous admiration for her dynamism, masked by a deceptively languid manner, and for the brilliant way she had adapted French methods to English materials and needs.

Late in 1945, Constance proposed to Miss Hume what was, in effect, a partnership. She had managed to rent premises in Victoria Street to re-start the flower school; she suggested that Miss Hume's cookery school should be re-started alongside, both of them offering full professional courses, and aiming to qualify for recognition by the Ministry of Education. Further, she was determined to form a residential country-house school of home-making, as soon as a suitable house could be found; cookery would be its principal subject, and for this too Miss Hume was invited to be responsible. After many long and anxious week-end discussions at Parkgate, Miss Hume agreed.

It meant, of course, that the Sprys would have to give up Parkgate, which was too small for a school, but would be too large and costly to run, Constance declared, once Shav retired. This came hard on him, for he loved the place, and could probably have afforded it very well if he had had a mate who was willing to stay quietly at home and look after him. But as usual, he was willing to fall in with any plan which furthered the exercise of her talents. It was in fact he who, through a house-agent's advertisement, found Winkfield Place.

It was a pleasant, rambling Georgian house with a large stable block, midway between Windsor and Ascot, just the sort of neighbourhood required. There was a large and intrinsically rather melancholy garden, bisected by a broad oblong lake, almost a wide canal, and with plenty of space for commercial flower and picking sections. The price was low for the Windsor area even by 1945 standards, but the house's state of disrepair was daunting. It had been a military orthopaedic hospital during the war, the walls were pitted with dart-holes, and the ceilings with hooks where limbs had been strung up. With the war barely over, labour in short supply and materials virtually non-existent, its conversion into a habitable house, let alone a school, appeared impossible to everyone but Constance. She knew immediately that Winkfield Place was what she needed, and in her determination to secure it, did what she had never been willing to do before, marched into her bank, and demanded and obtained a loan.

She had found her warden for the new school before the year was out. She was still giving her lectures, and one of them was to patients in a services hospital at Fulmer. It was preceded by an excellent lunch, and Constance, knowing that the hospital was soon to close, suggested to the head cook that she might become a teacher in the London cookery school. Mrs Dickie was interviewed by Rosemary Hume, who turned her down. But Constance continued to brood over the pretty young woman with a great gentleness of manner, which did not conceal an inner authority, and to feel that this was exactly the contrast she needed with the formidable headmistresses of her own youth. Presently she reappeared, and bore Christine Dickie over to Winkfield, where they explored the half-derelict mansion – 'she chiefly looked at the garden and I at the house,' Christine Dickie recalls – and made her proposition. The house was to become a place where school leavers and girls from the Forces would come for a year; it would not be a finishing school, but rather a 'beginning school', for those growing up in the next batch of wives and mothers. They would learn serious cookery, and house-keeping, and home decoration, and flower arrangement, and gardening, and book-binding, and fine needlework. And would Mrs Dickie come as its warden?

Constance would be the headmistress, but as she was not proposing to give up any of her other activities, a good many of the activities which usually fall to headmistresses would be delegated, such as the interviewing of parents who were not already personal friends of Mrs Spry, and the day to day administration, and the discipline. Christine Dickie had never done anything of the sort before, and she was understandably diffident. But her fears were laughed away in Constance's usual manner, and when the hospital closed, Mrs Dickie joined the circle of staff and friends desperately labouring on the making of curtains and bedspreads at Parkgate.

The readying of Winkfield was Constance's most brilliant feat of improvisation. The beds and much of the other furnishings were American war surplus, but she insisted that the effect was to be of young girls' bedrooms, not of school dormitories. They used butter muslin, parachute fabric, rolls of braid stitched together, any unrationed textiles that they could find. Fortunately most of the big ground-floor rooms had shutters, which served for a time instead of curtains, and for the drawing-room there were the patchwork curtains which Constance had for years been making out of the bits from Victor Stiebel's pre-war work-room. For its floor there was the needlework carpet, and for the other rooms and the corridors the carpeting was bomber felt. Bettie Smail claims the credit for suggesting that this should be dyed bright yellow, and the golden carpets are what everyone remembers about the early years at Winkfield, 'like sunshine on the floor'.

Walter Trower was warned that in June he would again have a garden to move: and in case the precious 'old' rose bushes did not transplant, Constance visited Hilling's nursery, where there was already a collection, to arrange for having slips of them propagated. Thus began one of her closest horticultural friendships, with Graham Stuart Thomas, who was then its manager. He realized at once that she knew far more about old roses than he did. The elaborate French names came rolling off her tongue, with perfect pronunciation, to the astonishment of the nursery workers.

At flowering time, she invited him down to Parkgate, and it was a revelation. In the garden were bushes of a size and magnificence he has never seen surpassed, and at least half-a-dozen varieties no one else had, not Robert James, nor Leonard Messel, nor Vita Sackville-West. On the lunch table, an enormous bowl of violet, lilac, purple and maroon roses spilled on to a pale green satin cloth. 'I felt,' he said, 'that here was a horticultural background I hadn't explored at all.' From then on they were in constant touch, and eventually he came to live not far from her. She was not an artist-gardener as he is, but she had much to teach him in the appreciation of the individual plant.

'How can you bear to leave?' said the friends who stayed at Parkgate that last summer; among them was Helen Kirkpatrick, now stationed in Paris, who came over to spend a last holiday in the lovely old house. It looked so perfect, and Winkfield still looked so desolate, filled with workmen straight out of the Army who had not yet had time to learn their trades fully, and who had to be shown, or persuaded, or harried, or cajoled by Constance as she went from room to room.

And when it was found that the splendid collection of antique furniture was going, not into some separate Spry residential quarter, but into the sitting-room which would be used by 'a set of grubby little schoolgirls', there was an outcry. It would be unappreciated, ruined, kicked to death.

Patiently, Constance explained that the most important

formative influence at Winkfield was to be a beautiful house. Girls who had come from the austerity of war-time schoolrooms, or from the hideousness of barracks and Nissen huts, were to spend a year in a place where everything they saw and used was elegant. Let it suffer if it must; but she did not think it would.

In fact, though she was such an avid collector, such a caressing admirer of objects, Constance had in her very little sense of personal possessiveness, and nothing at all of the hoarder. She would sell, or give away, some vase which she had used for years, when suddenly her eye went stale and it no longer provided her with inspiration. She scarcely cared where she slept or kept her clothes. For the first two years at Winkfield, the Sprys lived in a rented house across the road, and when a flat over the stables was at length contrived for them, Constance's bedroom was just another sitting-room, with a divan bed in one corner. She had lived much more grandly at Parkgate, but perhaps its very perfection had caused her to tire of it; it belonged to a phase of her life that was over. There was a good deal of the nomad in her. Her houses were like the silken tents of some Arab chief, hung with priceless carpets, but liable to vanish overnight.

Winkfield was her last camping-place, partly because she was old when she went there, but chiefly because it made possible for her a new type of creative activity. Far from being perfect, it was never finished. A new classroom was constantly being thrust out here, a new greenhouse put up there, a veranda glassed in to make a conservatory. Most of these additions were, architecturelly speaking, regrettable. Winkfield is a most enjoyable house, because so much goes on there, but Georgian mansions are seldom improved by being turned into schools, and in this it is no exception.

Winkfield is an object-lesson in owning possessions creatively, instead of gloating over them, or displaying them as museum pieces, or (worst counsel of despair) locking them away in banks. In the main, Constance's faith has been justified, and the young things who for nearly thirty years have trooped in and out of the house have put no more than a slight patina of shabbiness on the lovely furniture they are privileged to use. Some of her own adaptations may shock the antique trade; was it justifiable to thrust wire netting into the gilt font or turn the genuine Louis xv table into a jardiniere? But no matter; these things have been the materials for an artist, have been immortalized by pen and camera; they have been kept alive.

Her most famous vases are kept in a cupboard nowadays, but still brought out for the big occasions, like the party at the end of the summer term. And even when out of use they are not dead. One opens the cupboard and looks at them – the ormolu basket supported by two swans, the marble tazzas, the snake-twined blue and white glass urns, the bluejohn pieces that were Shav Spry's Christmas presents – and her spirit hovers over them still.

At the end of June, 1946, they moved into a house that was barely furnished. One's bed might be a grand four-poster and one's bedside table a soap-box. There were the inevitable disasters, such as discovering dry rot under the drawing-room floor after the decoration was finished, so that the workmen had to come back again. Everyone, whatever their ostensible functions, found themselves paintbrush in hand, including two new recruits, Daphne Holden, the last in Constance's line of secretaries, and Barbara Oakley, who had taken a course in interior decorating on coming out of the Forces, and was to teach that subject in the school.

It was vital to get the big and beautiful kitchen decorated, and Barbara Oakley, with a German ex-prisoner who had elected to stay on in Britain, worked on it for the whole of an exhausting week, with Constance's praise and gratitude to dispel their fatigue. In the evenings, she would talk to them about her plans. The disillusioned ex-officers on her staff urged her to make the discipline tough; she waved the notion aside, 'It will be all right, you'll see,' she told them. 'It always is if you're nice to people.' And after all, she knew something about the girls in the Forces. She had lectured to them, and shown them how to decorate their Nissen huts with flowers, and knew that they responded, like the children at Homerton, to any element of beauty introduced into their lives.

It suddenly struck someone that although she drove herself and them so hard, she was not well. Helen Kirkpatrick had had a curious experience in London; she had gone with a friend to a clairvoyant, not as a believer, rather to demonstrate to the friend that the old woman was probably a fraud. The clairvoyant said: 'Tell the friend you are staying with that the tumour she suspects she has won't turn out to be malignant'. As this did not apply to Miss Kirkpatrick's London hostess, she recounted the incident to Constance, who reluctantly admitted that she had a swelling, and that her masseuse had thought it might be a tumour.

Her dread of doctors and operations was as strong as ever, but this reassurance, coupled with Shav Spry's entreaties, at last persuaded her to see a specialist. She went into the Radcliffe Infirmary in Oxford at the end of August, and sure enough a non-malignant tumour was found, 'as big as a football.' 'I'll be back in time for the opening,' she had told them, and she was, though still very tottery, and obliged to take to her bed again immediately afterwards. This was her only serious illness till the day she died.

But in spite of this setback, her joy in her 'twenty-seven daughters', as she called them and as they came to call themselves, was great. This first intake were older than subsequent ones, and more intensely appreciative of the lovely surroundings in which they found themselves, and she got to know them intimately, as she could hardly do in later years when the school reached its complement of a hundred and twenty students. She even undertook a little teaching, taking on the salad-making class. But her real function was to teach them how to live, and here they were as clueless as she had expected. In an early exercise, she asked them to imagine themselves being entertained by a rich host at a grand restaurant; what food would they choose? None of them could get further than chicken with peas, and ice-cream.

They taught her much in return. They loved cooking and flower arrangement (Winkfield still suffers from being thought of as 'that place where they spend a year learning to do the flowers', though in fact it only occupies a tiny part of the curriculum), but they were bored by gardening. Over this she had been misled, both by her own enthusiasm, and by that of the Swanley students, who had chosen it as a career. Few of them were interested in fine needlework, and the class was switched to dressmaking and fashion. Miss Oakley's home decorating classes were a riotous success, and valuable as long as there were still empty rooms waiting to be decorated, but they had to be dropped in subsequent years because it proved quite impossible, in a house so bursting at the seams, to put rooms out of action for long periods while people learned to hang wallpaper.

And even the daughters of the affluent desired a wage-earning skill which would emancipate them from parental control; this was a development for which Constance had not quite budgeted. Accordingly, a secretarial course was added, while those who showed a real aptitude for cookery were enabled to stay on an extra term and take it to a professional standard.

But the principal aim was that they should learn to run civilized homes. They planned menus, marketed, cooked, and served the resulting meal to Mr and Mrs Spry and their guests, and as Constance adored entertaining, there was always a flow of appreciative guests of both sexes, to whom the young things could show off their skill. There were several big parties a year, to learn the doing of things in the grand manner: a harvest party on the scrubbed table of the kitchen, heaped with fruits and glowing red flowers; an elegant party for Ascot Gold Cup day, when the dining-room with its gold walls and yellow carpet was complemented by syringa and regale lilies, and by green cucumber soup and curried chicken, or other food 'toning' as exquisitely as it tasted. And there was the enormous passing-out party, attended by parents, and with Mr Stiebel's mannequins putting on a dress show; even when, in later years, the guest list mounted to several hundred, Constance always insisted that everyone should sit down to a proper meal.

What the girls wanted to learn, that they were given; what they felt to be out of tune with their post-war lives, she was ready to amend. On one point only did she yield with reluctance; they were not grateful to her, as she had expected, for freeing them from the tyranny of examinations. They wanted examinations, or at any rate some kind of a test at the end of the course, with a certificate of achievement, They wished to compete, and were unconcerned about the corollary, that where there is competition there are also going to be losers. This was the same ogre that Constance was to encounter in the flower-club movement, and once again she would fail to slay it.

An educationist who does not budget for so basic an urge in human nature may, perhaps, be considered naïve. Nevertheless, it is Constance's merit that though the event proved her mistaken as a teacher, as an artist she was perfectly right. And something of her attitude did rub off on her students, however little they may have realized it at the time. Looking back, they will acknowledge that what has remained with them is not the attaining of a diploma or certificate, but the joy and zest Mrs Spry communicated in doing something for its own sake, to satisfy one's own taste and judgment – and let the opinion of the world go hang.

Winkfield was now the hub of Constance's activities, but it was certainly not her livelihood. Although the fees seemed high, they came nowhere near running the house to the standard she exacted, and until the last year of her life, when it paid a modest dividend, the school was subsidized by the profits of the flower shop.

Her faculty for keeping six balls in the air at once seemed to increase with the years. The day-to-day running of the shop could be left to the returned stalwarts, and to a gifted new generation of decorators headed by Evelyn Russell and Jill Waring, but Constance visited it weekly, her arrival always sending electric waves through the staff, and if any arrangement particularly pleased her, she would ask who had done it and bestow her cherished praise. For any major event – for instance, the flowers in Westminster Abbey for the marriage of Princess Elizabeth and Prince Philip, which was the firm's first big royal commission – she still headed the designing team.

She lectured to the London cookery and flower schools two or three times every term, and bestowed the end-of-course certificates. She lectured all over the country in support of the growing flower-club movement, of which more presently. She had accepted that demonstrations were henceforward to be a required part of a flower talk, though she would never do them herself; she spoke first, to her slides, and then Mrs Russell or Miss Waring would demonstrate, while she sat in the front row and sewed away at her latest piece of tapestry – for her hands were never idle. They remember her particular delight in the lecture trips to Ireland; once aboard the boat her worries fell from her. Her base in Dublin was usually Lady Moore's house and famous garden at Rathfarnham, and the lectures were hilariously interspersed with lunch parties, visits to gardens and the renewing of old friendships. George Fletcher's daughter was never forgotten in Ireland, and it is not surprising that the myth of her Irish origin steadily grew.

She lectured to the day courses for outsiders held at Winkfield in term-time, and the week-end or week ones which kept the house lively during the school holidays. That these should supplement her work with young girls had been part of her plan from the beginning, as her letters show. They would, she explained, be a way of paying part of the running expenses. But in fact the fees charged were modest, and a wide cross-section of housewives, from London and from the residential districts within reach of Windsor, came, as they still do, to enjoy the beauty of the house and to have their cookery and flower-arranging skills brushed up.

In some ways they were more rewarding than the girls, for their interest was already there, it did not have to be awakened. Even to the woman who could only manage a day visit, it meant a cookery class in the morning, a flower class in the afternoon, congenial company, and a delicious lunch she had not had to cook herself. For thousands it has been a refreshment of mind and body, a grand day-out, and Constance as hostess and principal speaker remains in their memories, particularly if it were in June or July, when she would make her characteristic entrance, arms loaded with old roses.

She always had a book on the stocks. The twin volumes of *Summer and Autumn Flowers* (May 1951), and *Winter and Spring Flowers*, (November of the same year), celebrate her joyous recapture of gardening delights after the austerities of war. As before, the emphasis is first on growing, with picking as a bonus. She is eager to point out how many things, even the exotic ones, are within the scope of most purses, 'a millionaire for a few pence' in the phrase she borrowed from V. Sackville-West; the open ground provides something to pick all through the year, but of course, if there is a little greenhouse, one can do marvels. Herself still continually making discoveries, she communicates her excitement. And it is not a pose. With all that she had on her hands at Winkfield, she still found time and had the physical strength to go out and tussle with that intractable soil, 'in the wet weather you could model a statue out of it, in dry weather a gardener's cottage cracked along with it.' She would bring in a single flower or spray for minute study, and it was this in a glass, not a lavish 'Spry arrangement', that she commonly kept on her desk.

For the first time in her books, she was able to use coloured illustrations, She had no faith in colour photography, still in its crude stage, and chose instead to have black and white photographs coloured by hand – a compromise not entirely satisfactory, but which does give some idea of the subtleties of colour she achieved. There are the slaty pinks and purples of the old roses; or hellebores from the garden, wild daphne from the woods and bilbergia from the greenhouse to startle the early spring with pink and lime green; or an autumn combination of berries, callicarpa, blackberry, vitis, to pick up the colours of a bluejohn urn. No doubt many have copied these notions since, but Constance thought of them first.

In addition to the books, there was a flow of articles for magazines and newspapers, which continually requested Mrs Spry's views on this and that, notably at Chelsea time, when also she made contributions to radio programmes on gardening. The post-war Chelsea shows were, as we all remember, a quite angry riot of colour, with 'bigger and brighter therefore better' as the keynote, and Mrs Spry did not always endear herself to the trade by speaking up for a gentle display of herbs, or of the subtle oncocyclus irises, or of the new tulips being bred from *viridiflora*, their sides streaked with pale green.

Always inventive, she had days when the creative ideas would seem to come bursting out of her, and everyone knew the signs; she would grow abstracted, and her thick, springy hair would literally stand on end. Then she would need all her 'black boys' to help her carry them out, to draw and paint and gum and glitter, and twist wire and fabric, perhaps till two in the morning. 'Oh why haven't you got a third hand?' she would wail, or with compunction: 'You don't mind, darling, do you?' One was not supposed, ever, to say no when Constance had a creative fit, and it took a good while to be forgiven if one did.

Complete strangers would be roped in. Daphne Holden recalls the first visit to Winkfield of her mother, who was handed a sheet of paper and asked to draw a birdcage. She explained regretfully that she had no drawing skill. 'Nonsense,' said Constance briskly, 'anyone can draw a birdcage.' The fact that she herself could not draw anything was neither here nor there. Mrs Holden sat down and for two hours struggled with this very tricky exercise in perspective, at the end of which she had produced a creditable drawing of a birdcage.

And this was partly the secret of Constance's enormous activity. She had the gift, rare among women, of knowing how to delegate, without ever herself being superseded. She gathered round her the talented, and developed and controlled their talents, almost without appearing to do so. There are solitary creatures, and social ones, and Constance was decidedly of the latter kind. She worked in and through other people, and in doing so, enabled them to find fulfilment. It was very seldom, in point of fact, that anyone wished to say no.

'Of course she was a slave-driver,' Daphne Holden says. 'We were worked into the ground. But goodness, how we laughed! We've never laughed like that since she died.'

The private quarters contrived for the Sprys in the stable block at Winkfield were modest enough; a small dining-room on the ground floor, and above it, reached by a steep little staircase, two sitting-rooms and a bedroom. But Constance's possessions and taste quickly filled them with enchanting objects, and one of the sitting-rooms was panelled with the grey mirror glass from Atkinson's shop. The firm had changed hands, Norman Wilkinson's lovely decor had been scrapped, and Constance had bought the glass, the stock of vases, and the fountain, which for a time functioned at South Audley Street, till too many people tripped over it. The work of her dead friend and teacher formed a delicate setting for herself.

Private the apartments scarcely were, as Constance's love of her 'daughters' meant that they and the staff and endless visitors could penetrate to her at all times of the day. Shav Spry endured it with his usual good humour, and took the same fatherly interest in the young ladies of the school as he had done in those of the shop, but it was not an ideal background for an elderly man who had earned a retirement of peace and quiet. He loved country life, and the country round Winkfield is not immediately inspiring. Finally he rented – to his regret he was never allowed to buy – a rambling white house called Ard Daraich, on the western shore of Loch Linnhe, with a breathtaking view across the water to Ben Nevis and the mountains of Glencoe.

Here he spent all but the winter months, and here Val Pirie created for him the moorland garden, painfully fashioned from bare hummocky hillside, to which Constance devotes a lyrical chapter in the last of her flower books. She would join him at the end of each summer term, accompanied by as many of the 'black boys' as she could inviegle into a working holiday, and in the relaxing peace and beauty of Ard Daraich would get much of her writing done. She would take gentle walks up and down the road, or do a little boating on the loch, but her favourite diversion was to go off by car and spend a night at Inverness, where she and Spry had discovered an antique shop stuffed with treasures at a fraction of London prices. Vanloads of inlay and carving and marquetry went south to Winkfield in due course. (This situation, I hasten to add, no longer obtains; Scottish antique dealers are perfectly *au fait* with market prices today.)

Of course she missed her husband when he was not in residence at Winkfield. She had always relished masculine company, and the predominantly feminine atmosphere in the house would now and then get on her nerves. Then there would be frantic telephone calls to her men friends: 'You must come and save my life, come to lunch and spend the day.' The rescuer would probably find himself one of a party when he arrived.

She talked gardening with Graham Thomas and Beverley Nichols and Roy Hay, decorating and antique-hunting with Hermann Schrijver and Oliver Messel and Victor Stiebel; but most of all, when the young ladies on duty for the day had assured the service and left her alone with her guests, she enjoyed swapping Rabelaisian stories, a taste which surprised and delighted them, particularly as it accorded so little with her soft voice and gentle manner. Her own contributions could be very funny when she was on form, and even funnier if she lost the thread or was overcome by embarrassment half-way through. It was the same when she went visiting; the host would be deputed before lunch to show her the herbaceous border, and presently there floated back to the hostess gales of laughter which had nothing to do with the delphiniums.

In the nature of things, most of Constance's original stories have vanished, but Roy Hay recalls one of her favourites, about being interviewed on a radio programme in America.

'Oh, Mrs Spry,' gushed the woman interviewer, 'we over here do so love your English flowers, and most of all your cute pansies, with their soft little faces and their lovely long stalks.' American women journalists are not a naïve race, and one can't help wondering whether one of them really made the remark, or whether Constance merely thought it would have been rather fun if she had.

8. FLOWERS FOR EVERYONE

The growth of Winkfield as a centre of cultural diffusion, and of the flower-arrangement societies, conveniently and happily coincided. Classes for vases of flowers at village produce shows were not, of course, anything new; they went back at least to Gertrude Jekyll's day; but they took a back place, and the standard was usually low. Constance's influence and the impact of her books and lectures were causing it to be taken seriously, even before the founding of the first specialist society. Women's movements, and particularly the Women's Institutes and the Townswomen's Guilds, were including it in their programmes, and Sheila Macqueen and others were busy training lecturer-demonstrators in the Spry technique.

There had been an all-arrangement show at Cheltenham before the war, about which little seems to be remembered. The real beginning of the club movement can be dated from a show in the Dorchester Corn Exchange in June 1950. Its genesis was as follows. Major J. M. B. Wratislaw of Yeovil, organizer of the Dorset County Produce Association and a prominent land-owner, had had the idea of improving the performance at county shows by forming a panel of demonstrators and judges, and Mrs Cecil Pope of Dorchester became one of its members. She, like Adele Lovett in New York, was a Constance Spry in embryo. She owned a large and beautiful garden which was her passion, arranged flowers in the Dutch manner, had a Constance-like facility for collecting rare containers, and had travelled in America and Canada and been impressed by the display technique of their arrangement shows. And she was a pretty young woman, in whom charm went with organizing ability and drive.

She suggested to the panel that a society devoted wholly to flower decoration should be formed; its inaugural meeting was at Dorchester in December of 1949. Shortly before this, Constance had been lecturing at Yeovil; members of the panel told her what was going forward, and she expressed interest, but also some doubt, particularly as to whether members would really enjoy having their arrangements criticized. Invited to become the new society's patron, she replied: 'I don't think it will work, but I'll give you a year, and I'll be your patron if you're still going at the end of it.'

In the event, she did not have to wait that long. The first show was mounted in the following June; she came down, and was enraptured. Here was just the spontaneous expression of delight in flowers, shared by all social classes, which she had longed to see. Over three hundred exhibits filled the great hall of the Dorchester Corn Exchange, and it seemed to her that there was not an ugly one among them. Mary Pope, with American methods in mind, had contrived the system of seperate display niches which is now a commonplace, but which was then new to Britain. Undulating strips of corrugated cardboard were run the length of the show benches, and the cardboard had been painted white, but the white was mixed with a little apple-green, which softened it and gave a pearly background, showing up the flowers to the happiest advantage.

The exhibits were of all types and sizes, from noble flower pieces suited to the rooms of West Country mansions, through jugs and bowls holding cottage bunches, down to true miniatures. A special section was devoted to children's flowers, and Mrs Pope had had the schools and teachers' training colleges circulated beforehand, so that there should be wide encouragement to take part. As well as individual vases, there were group efforts by school classes: a party table with a miniature maypole in the centre, gardens made on plates and trays, dolls' houses with flowers arranged in perfect proportion in each room. The children had not been fobbed off with jamjars, as so often happened at the ordinary horticultural show; trouble had been taken to supply them with containers as graceful as any used by their elders.

And the whole affair was non-competitive; that, to Constance, was the greatest merit of all. There were no prizes, no medals or ribbons, no descending order of merit. People had got up with the dawn, and travelled miles with their impedimenta, not in order to come first or second, but simply to join in a great festival of self-expression through flowers. And this seemed to Constance to prove her point, that flower arrangement was a true art and not just another parlour-game. The Dorset village woman, picking a bunch from her garden and arranging it in a jug, could achieve something as satisfying in its way, as 'suitable' to use the favourite Spry adjective of praise, as the more sophisticated Dorchester or Yeovil townswoman who had looked at Dutch flower paintings, or at the books of Mrs Spry. Constance had a warm appreciation of country folk and their instinctive rightness of touch; she had a way of noticing them at her lectures, and would seek them out afterwards, break through their shyness, get them talking about their gardens, as like as not ask for their advice.

The children's share also delighted her, and the pattern set for children's classes, dish-gardens, teacup posies, collections of wild flowers and so on, has been generally followed since.

Dorchester's success fired others; three more societies rapidly came into being, in London, Leicester and Colchester. (Constance was guest of honour at the inaugural Leicester meeting under the presidency of the Mayoress, Isobel Barnett, not yet famous as a television personality; she was to become a close friend.) Two years after the Dorset show, these first four societies staged the first 'Floral Academy', the Royal Horticultural Society lending them its New Hall free of charge, and the President, Lord Aberconway, honouring them by opening the event. Once again, there were no prizes. Mary Pope in her advance notice to the press explained:

'It will not be in any way like an orthodox flower show, nor will it be competitive. It is felt that where flower decoration is competitive, the full beauty of the individual arrangements is often lost to the public by the unavoidable comparison with other exhibits. In such events, people tend eagerly to seek out the first, second and third prize exhibits, and in their enthusiasm for comparison, are moved to judge the class themselves – thereby very often missing the individual beauty and grace of any particular exhibit or even missing the whole purpose of its design.'

Constance was present as the only kind of judge she liked to be, not placing in order of merit but offering constructive criticism. At Dorchester she had been nervous to offer anything but praise, but now that they had convinced her that her advice was valued, she took infinite pains to write little comments on each exhibit. Many of these are treasured still.

The London show was far more widely seen than the Dorchester one, and emulation followed fast; clubs sprang up all over the country. Most of the founders were strongly Spry-influenced, like Dora Buckingham, the moving spirit in Berkshire, who had taken a course at the Flower School in its early days, had returned for a refresher after the war, and was among Constance's most fervent admirers. Constance herself opened, judged, lectured with untiring enthusiasm, and usually for free. 'Mrs Spry's high fees proved illusory as she did not charge any,' is the sort of comment I find.

The first tent devoted solely to flower arrangement at the Chelsea Show was in May of 1956; the first decorating of a Stately Home was at Montacute House in July of the same year, in aid of the National Trust, and a photographic calendar of the groups which has survived shows them to have been magnificent. The first church to be given the full treatment of decoration as a fund-raising attraction was the Abbey Church of Milton Abbas, in 1957, and £350 was raised for its fabric fund. These events proved that the public would pay to see flower decoration, and what was more, would queue, to an extent hardly inspired by any other aesthetic spectacle. When Westminster Abbey was decorated, people waited for two hours to get in, and the arrangement tent at Chelsea is now the biggest draw. A valuable new form of fund-raising had been found.

In January of 1959 the National Association of Flower Arrangement Societies of Great Britain was formed, with Mary Pope as its first president. In October of that year, the pioneer Dorset society celebrated its tenth anniversary, with an exhibition again opened by Constance.

She had become godmother to a triumphant mass movement. But like most mass movements, it carried within itself elements which the founders had not envisaged, and which were not wholly in accordance with their ideas.

For although the founders were as anxious as Constance to keep the competitive element out, this proved no more possible than it had been at Winkfield. The great majority of members of what was a thoroughly democratic movement wished to pit their skills against each other, and to be told who had come out on top, and naturally their will prevailed. Constance acknowledges as much in the second half of her 'Flower Show' chapter, already quoted, when she suggests show classes and schedules, some of them taken from what she had observed in America, and urges that there should be classes reserved for those who have never before taken a prize.

Her suggestions generally are as sensible as one would expect, and leave plenty of scope for the individual to express herself; yet even here there are items she must soon have regretted, since they opened the way to abuses she was soon to deplore.

She suggests groups for different types of room, well and good; then a group to be called 'Yesteryear' or 'Romance' or 'Nostalgia'. But if flowers can be used to express any 'theme' other than their own nature, they can be used to express catch phrases or the titles of popular songs, as indeed they very soon were. She suggests arrangements accompanied by pieces of fabric or needlework, or a small statue or other decorative object, to give the illusion that they are standing in a room, an illusion in any case impossible within the restricted niche which is all the average show allows; the result has been the rash of 'drapes' and 'accessories' which appear to turn flower arrangement into an extension of window-dressing. She suggests an arrangement inspired by a picture or a poem, which is merely a confusing of unrelated art-forms. It is the more curious because none of these were things she ever did herself, or allowed her learners to do.

But she was terribly anxious that the movement should succeed; she had immense sympathy with organisers and secretaries, nervous lest members' interest should flag. She was fully aware that what gives the art its lasting fascination is that the material itself is always new, and in a sense unpredictable; but she was not, perhaps, sufficiently confident that the beginner would find it so.

The National Association had felt itself, inevitably, obliged to formulate rules for judges and competitors, and had done so with anxious care, intending them for general guidance. Too often, they were taken *au pied de la lettre*. Constance's visitors to the outside courses at Winkfield would exclaim with pleasure at her great bowls of roses, dripping on to satin tablecloths, 'but we wouldn't be allowed to do anything like that,' they told her. Why not? 'Because table flowers must be low and they mustn't touch the table.' Who said so? 'Oh, it says so in the rules.' It was what she had already seen in America, the formula fossilizing, the spontaneity lost.

Most of all, she found herself repelled by the short cuts which the very eagerness and urgency of the movement's growth were imposing on teachers and learners. It was certainly possible to find an A-line or an S-line in a Dutch flower-painting, or for that matter, in a Spry group – though Constance herself was never very fond of the S, of which she says merely: 'With a few flowers, one may be helped by arranging them in this line.' And if the A, which was her most usual outline, appeared too obvious, she would apologize for 'a somewhat overstated triangle'. But these effects were achieved mainly by instinct, and by following the nature of the material. To turn them into geometric dodges was to make real flowers look like artificial ones – as, it might be claimed, a good many prizewinning compositions do to this day.

There are no short-cuts in any art, however minor; it must always be the expression of the artist's talent and cultural background. Constance had taken gifted boys and girls with little or no cultural background, and turned them into artists, but they had learned from her, slowly and lovingly, absorbing the look of her houses and gardens and ornaments, the way she did things, the way her senior decorators did things, the effect created in this or that church or ballroom, analysed, criticized, discussed. And now hundreds of women, many of whom had

scarcely looked at a picture or at a garden, or bought a beautiful thing for their houses, were being encouraged to believe
that they could get there quickly by taking a few measurements,
building up a geometric outline, and following the rules.

Not only was it not the way, she felt; it undid whatever in-
born feeling for beauty they might have. The countrywoman's
posy in a jug was artless, but it was charming; after all, the
French Impressionists honoured it often enough by painting it.
But give that same countrywoman a short course in 'floral art'
and the results were only too sadly likely to be non-U. (Incidentally, with her fastidious taste in words, Constance was not
over-fond of the adjective floral, particularly when applied to
the noun art, and anything calling itself a Floral Art Club had
to overcome a minor hurdle before it found its way to her
affections.)

She was awkwardly placed. She could not countenance the
vulgarities of the movement, and yet she loved it, and it loved
her. She was far and away the greatest name in flower arrangement, and the members were pathetically anxious for her com-
mendation; not was she ever much of a hand at hurting feelings
or dealing out snubs. 'Tell us what we do wrong,' they urged her,
by which they meant, tell us how to do it right. But she had
no short-cuts for them. 'Suitability' was her key-word, but it
was not very helpful. Telling people to do what is suitable is
like telling them to use their common-sense; if they could do
it, they would not need to be told.

'Study the growing plant, learn in the garden rather than
in the floral art class,' she suggested, and indeed it is the lesson
throughout her books; no other writer of a series of flower
arrangement books has devoted anything like the space to pure
gardening. It was unsuitable to put grapes with daffodils,
because they could never be out at the same time, but it was
allowable to put lemons with small white narcissi because the
trees of the citrus family bear last year's fruit and this year's
small white flowers together. But then, not everyone had a
garden, and not everyone, at any rate in those days, could
spend holidays in Hammamet.

So she continued to visit, and lecture, and judge, her judgments often saying for her what she could not say outright.

When the other members of the panel pointed out that the piece she favoured broke this rule or that, 'I could live with it,' she would answer; she was the great Constance Spry, and that was that. Or usually; but she was sometimes challenged. George Foss wryly recalls an occasion when she had to judge a class 'interpreting *Swan Lake*.' One competitor had with infinite labour unpicked a hundred white carnations to make a large swan and set it on a piece of mirror, and when the results were known she pursued Constance across the hall, shouting furiously: 'Why didn't you give me the prize?' He tried simultaneously to soothe the outraged lady and shield the terrified Constance, whose fault, indeed, it was; she should never have lent herself to the judging of a section 'interpreting *Swan Lake*'. And after a while, she did withdraw from judging panels in classes she considered ill-advised; she would explain smilingly that on this particular branch of floral art, she did not feel herself competent to speak.

Harder to bear was the ridicule which such excesses brought not only on the movement, but upon Constance as its figurehead, and for a long time the only name known to the outside world. And though in the final instance she cared very little for the opinions of kings and princes, with the kings and princes of horticulture she did wish to stand well. When Brigadier Lucas-Phillips or Mr Will Ingwersen denounced the silliness of flower arrangement in the horticultural press, she was stung, though once they had got to know her, they easily recognized that her art was complementary to theirs, and that she deplored its misuse as much as they did. To Will Ingwersen in July of 1958 she writes: 'You will hardly believe that only last week, I saw a rose dressed up with a blue crinoline of heads of delphinium, with pins stuck in to represent eyes, and labelled *My Fair Lady*. I do so dislike these interpretative classes, and I cannot see any charm or any beauty in them.'

But it would be quite unfair to give the impression that Constance's relations with the flower-club movement were in the main unhappy. She rejoiced in its spread and successes, she made allowance for its difficulties; she knew that the pioneer leaders felt as she did on almost all points, even if they could not outrun the views of the membership. The criticisms she voices in *Favourite Flowers* are put with her usual gentleness, and seasoned by a disarming disclaimer:

'I expect I have irritated many whom I have no wish to annoy, and I certainly have offered myself a very perfect sacrifice to the winners of medals and trophies, who might fairly point out that I have never won anything and am hardly qualified therefore to talk about criticism.' One can see her smiling as she writes these last words.

From the beginning, the clubs had looked for work they could do to beautify public places, churches and hospitals particularly, as an act of service to the community. And here, the value of the non-competitive approach was triumphantly proved. The work done grew progressively better, so that it is hard to credit that the same people could produce these lovely groups and the horrid little whimsies in the competitive niches; yet in many cases it must have been true. The reasons are plain enough. Firstly, the church or hospital flowers were in a setting, and no decorative art can be satisfactorily practised separate from its setting. Then, the arrangers followed Constance's advice that the intrinsic beauty of the building should be enhanced, not obscured; or, if it were an ugly one, that the flowers should distract attention from its ugly features, not attempt to cover them up.

But principally, the club members were heeding the admonition continually urged upon them by Mary Pope, that when they arranged flowers in churches (or for that matter, in hospitals or schools or prisons), they must work for the glory of God and not for their own. And such an approach almost automatically got rid of what Constance had called 'affectation, pretentiousness, and tricks generally.' Indeed, I suppose it may be said that all real artists work primarily for the glory of God and not for their own, whether or no they have a formal religious faith. It is not to be supposed that Henry Moore deliberately sets out to do 'better' than Barbara Hepworth, or Picasso than Matisse.

Constance's approval was fully disinterested, in that the public decorating done by the flower societies was in direct competition with her own trade. To the retail flower trade it has brought nothing but good, though it took a little time for this to be realized. But jobs of decorating could not be achieved entirely from the members' own gardens; much more was bought, at members' expense. That the trade has reciprocated by providing them with more varied and beautiful material can hardly be maintained. As has been noted, the trend is towards fewer and more stereotyped lines in flowers, and as for foliage, the position has been summed up by Sybil Emberton, a contemporary expert, as 'grow it or go without'.

But it was evident that as more and more women became able to decorate public buildings to a professional standard, a professional decorating business must lose some custom. Such a consideration did not weigh at all with Constance. Challenged, she always said that if flowers became an intrinsic part of everyday living, there would always be enough work, both amateur and professional, to keep everyone happy.

The reproach that might at first have been made to her, of working for the rich and mighty, had never really been justified; they were useful to her, as she to them. But now there was no sting in it. 'I do feel so strongly that flowers should be a medium of self-expression for everyone,' she had written. Before her death, the flower clubs, and the Women's Institutes and Townswomen's Guilds, and even the local authorities when they included flower arrangement in their further education courses, had begun to make her wish come true.

Constance had been acquainted with the Minister of Works, Mr David Eccles (as he then was), for many years. It was for Mrs Eccles' mother, Lady Dawson of Penn, that Flo Standfast had made the shell tiara which attracted King George v's approval. She knew that they were passionate gardeners, and had visited the lovely garden of their farmhouse near Andover. Moreover, she had had the honour of doing the Westminster Abbey flowers for the Queen's wedding. Nevertheless, it was with complete astonishment that she received the Minister's invitation to become his adviser on flowers for the Coronation processional route. In spite of her wide and growing fame, she had never considered this or that assignment as her due.

The Minister attached great importance to the embellishment of the route. It was, he knew, the only part of the ceremony in which Londoners and visitors would physically share; the guests in the Abbey would be the merest handful in comparison. The Festival of Britain had already shown, in the summer of 1951, that war-battered Britain could still do things with immense inventiveness, gaiety and style. The Coronation, adding the majesty and solemnity of a royal and religious occasion, would be an even greater opportunity.

He visualized an unbroken flow of decorations for the whole route, with flowers massed at key points along it. 'And I wasn't going to have them just wheel out the geraniums,' he says. To invite Constance Spry on to his team was the best way of ensuring that they did better than that. And to her, it was the crown of her career. She had a deep personal veneration for the Queen, 'that Byzantine figure', and the scope offered to her meant, as she wrote afterwards, months of the most exciting work that could ever have come a flower woman's way.

The rest of the team consisted of officials from the Ministry, all experts in their fields, and the reaction when they heard that an outsider was to join them was one of outrage. 'Over our dead bodies,' the Minister was told. He held firm, though warning Constance that she would find the going sticky at the preliminary meetings in the summer of 1952, and so it proved. At the start she was cold-shouldered and people would hardly speak to her. 'But she seduced them,' Lord Eccles recalls with a chuckle. The Fletcher charm operated still.

Not, of course, only the Fletcher charm; these were people far too intelligent to be won over by mere wheedling. They quickly came to respect her knowledge and flair, and to realize that with it went a genuine humble-mindedness, and that she had no wish to usurp the position which belonged of right to Eric Bedford, the Ministry's chief architect, as the overall designer of the route. She had much to teach them about flowers, but equally, much to learn from them about the techniques of decorating on a vast processional scale.

Nor was there any great divergence in their thinking. They all agreed with the Spry principle that flowers should be banked in blocks and drifts of colour, rather than in dots or straight lines, and that patriotism could be expressed without the stereotype of red, white and blue; that the heraldic colours of scarlet, pale blue and gold were much preferable; that white flowers, always difficult, were most effective when blocked together; that a blue scheme, enlivened with white, would be appropriate outside the Admiralty; that the parterres outside the Abbey Annexe might show the soft pinks and mauves of an English country garden in high summer. They were relieved to find that far from turning up her nose at the scarlet geraniums round the Queen Victoria Memorial, outside Buckingham Palace, so dear to the London heart, Mrs Spry proposed reinforcing them with thousands more, and with all the other red flowers – verbena, salvia, phlox drummondii – that could be found. A preliminary scheme was worked out, so that Mr W. J. Hepburn, the Superintendant of Parks, could put in hand the huge propagation programme necessary if his green-houses were to furnish the material required.

And Constance shortly found herself with another large undertaking on her hands. Crowned heads do not attend the coronations of others, but send their next-of-kin, and Presidents their deputies, and some three hundred of these august visitors were expected; on the Minister of Works lay the responsibility of offering them a luncheon at the conclusion of the service. (Government hospitality has been in charge of the Minister of Works since the days of George III, who, it is said, considered that the then holder of the office was the only man he could trust not to put the funds allocated into his own pocket.) It had been assumed that the function could be handed over to one of the hotels or large catering firms, but Mr Eccles found that he had underestimated the world-wide interest the occasion was arousing. Even at this early stage, every hotel was booked solid, every caterer had as much as he could manage on his hands, not an extra waiter was to be hired. He confided to Constance that he was at his wits' end.

'But let me and Rosemary Hume do it,' she said, 'and our students from Winkfield and the cookery school will do the waiting. You find us a room somewhere near the Abbey, and we'll do the rest.' Having by now complete faith in her powers, he accepted with relief. There was another outcry when the rest of the hospitality committee were told of his decision. 'You are entrusting the lunch to a set of amateurs and a cookery school,' he was told. But as no one had a practical alternative to offer, he felt justified in putting these objections aside.

The setting found was Up School, the great hall of Westminster School, originally the monks' dormitory of the Abbey. It had been a noble apartment, panelled, and with a great hammerbeam roof; roof and panelling had been destroyed in the blitz of 1941, and when Constance looked around she saw an ugly temporary ceiling, and very nearly the 'whitewashed barn' she had sometimes longed for when contemplating the overfurnished drawing-rooms of Mayfair. She says that a fit of nerves assailed her, and that someone using the word 'medieval' gave her the clue to the colours of an illuminated missal; but she is probably being modest, since such a scheme was already in her head for the processional flowers, and the room must have stirred her imagination much as a theatrical designer's is stirred by an empty stage.

In *Party Flowers*, she has described how she and Val Pirie put their heads together and evolved their plan: the long serving tables draped in gold, the small round luncheon tables given soft grey-blue tablecloths, the flowers in 'clashing reds', a bouquet of them on each table, set on a raised stand supporting a gold crown, and huge groups of them set at intervals rather high up round the walls, thereby distracting attention from the roof. The glittering uniforms and robes of the guests would do the rest.

By August, the Minister was able to outline his plans to the press, and to tell them that he had the co-operation of Mrs Spry; 'they murmured (this is equal to cheers in the House of Commons) their approval,' he wrote to her. The publicity attendant on anything connected with the event was more embarrassment than pleasure; more to her liking was the fact that she was now fully accepted as a member of the team, and even listened to on matters not directly concerned with flowers. Eric Bedford's brilliant design for 'lion and unicorn' arches over the Mall called for banners on each side, which would be seen against the yellow-green of the plane trees in young June leaf, and what colour to use for the banners was a puzzlement to all. Constance suggested two vertical panels in her beloved clashing reds; there was a moment of consternation; then she picked out two roses, in vermilion and in crimson, from a bowlful which the Minister had brought up from Andover and had on his table, and the point was made.

Overworked though he was, the Minister yet found time to scribble his thoughts to Constance, often in pencil and late at night; with his kind permission I quote from these letters, which give such a vivid idea not only of the high seriousness but of the almost boyish zest he brought to his task. (Unfortunately Constance's replies have not survived.)

Minister of Works to Constance Spry, 16 August 1952. 'You are quite right about plenty of gold. When I had the 1937 films run over I saw that white is a cuckoo of a colour and the enemy of good pictures. So I told my people to cut it out and put in gold whenever they could.

'The Department is in the dumps about gold ropes. It seems that for the thickness we want they cost 6s. 6d. a yard and we need 7000 yards (for the Mall principally.) They want therefore to give up ropes, but I am not yet satisfied that we need be beaten.'*

'The design and decoration of the Annexe to the Abbey are coming on well. I will try and do you a sketch, however badly. The colours will be red and gold with a blue lining to the top canopy. The roof of the lower canopy will be glass to help the cameras, and we must not put too much drapery as they want to get angle shots of the Queen alighting, etc.

'Running round the base of the Annexe we can have a hedge of flowers. Of course they want hydrangeas but I hanker for yellows. Anyway you can do a design and we'll put our heads together over it. I will let you have a coloured drawing of the Annexe as soon as one is ready, and then you will see your backcloth.

'I am very pleased with my notion to put a file of the Queen's Beasts – lions or unicorns – on the skyline of the west end of the Annexe. They will look at once medieval and a match for Mossadek.'

Minister of Works to Constance Spry, Christmas Eve, 1952. 'You have a special genius for pageants in miniature – the gift of perishable splendour.

> But oh! the very reason why
> I clasp them is because they die.

There's a flower-seller's song for you. Strange that England, who used to be in love with *fantaisie*, with poets and processions, has been now so long content to live on bread and rations. Our immediate fathers seem to have forgotten that the imagination is as powerful as the stomach. Our fantasy has been sleeping, but now it yawns and stretches, and if you and I pull the clothes off next June, it will get right out of bed. Only we have to navigate a new sort of imagination, a popular

---

* They were not beaten. Ordinary rope was bought, and treated with gold paint.

imagination flooding round the single lighthouse of the Throne, an imagination Commonwealth in extent and far simpler in quality than the Edwardian and Georgian mixture of peers, courtiers, and money-bags.

'You realize the risks we are taking in stoking up so early and so lustily the expectations of the common people? The higher we climb beforehand, the further we can fall on the day. But then who would not speculate all he has, and more, for the Queen?

'Our duty is to give her blossoming renown an outward and visible form significant to the popular imagination. If we made a mess of it, we should disappoint the hearts of millions. We might even be guilty of splintering the Commonwealth at the one and only moment allowed us to reverse the process of separation which has gone so far. And this chance must be taken with nothing better than the passive support of the Cabinet, whose thoughts are on the House of Commons and the daily conduct of State affairs, e.g. in all these months not one small suggestion for the Coronation preparations has come from either the Colonial or the Commonwealth Relations Offices. As far as I know, they may be quite indifferent to the influence of the pageant upon the lives and loyalties of those for whom they are responsible, or with whom they are the link with HMG.

'If, in all this, there is no cause for dismay, that must chiefly be because you are enlisted in our handful of "metteurs en scene". I believe in our team success. On Monday we will see what has to be decided in January.'

Minister of Works to Constance Spry, 6 April 1953. 'You know those corrugated tank-like structures which are lavatories, and are going up in the Parks. I won't have them blocks of Government green, and I have suggested stripes, blue and white (MEN) and pink and white (WOMEN), half the lav. in each. Then the public would quickly grasp the colour signal and we need not have such huge notices 'Gents' 'Ladies' etc. But I fear this is too frivolous for the Parks Director or MOW.

'I am going over the route all day on Thursday with Sir Charles Mole, to see about the timetable. It will give me an opportunity to have a look at the flower positions. Next week

I will try to get from the Parks just how many flowers we are going to have, I have sent for a breakdown of their Coronation budget (£15,000) which is a means of seeing what they are doing.'

All through the winter and spring, the Ministry's workshops were busy making (among countless other things) the golden crown baskets Constance and Mr Bedford had designed to hold great bouquets of plants in flower, hung high on standards along the route. (Another Spry maxim: keep the flowers high for a party.) And Constance's workshops were busy on the decorations for the luncheon room. The Minister had been voted a hospitality grant by the House of Commons, but there could be no question of extravagance, and rightly, the food and drink were to have priority. Constance had therefore ample scope to demonstrate once more her genius for improvisation.

The effect of gilded leather draperies down the length of the serving tables was got by using cheap plastic, and painting it in graded tones of gold (Evelyn Russell still remembers the wearisome hours of painting). The cloths for the luncheon tables were made from inexpensive furnishing taffeta in an exquisite blue, brighter than powder, deeper than ice. The table vases were round tins covered by gold crowns and mounted on curving metal legs. Surrounding each on the tablecloth was a garland of gold leaves, modelled by 'the arts'. The problem of finding enough red flowers was solved when the Mayor and citizens of San Remo offered a gift of flowers to the Queen; they were invited to concentrate on scarlets and pinks, using roses, carnations, gladioli and strelitzias in particular.

It was further announced that a huge gift of flowers would be coming from the Commonwealth countries, principally South Africa; these were to be used to decorate the Commonwealth stands in Parliament Square. The Royal Horticultural Society offered quantities of branches from flowering shrubs, chiefly rhododendron, azalea and lilac, from its gardens at Wisley. Everything could be and was used, for the amount of flowers required was prodigious. And Constance had agreed to yet another undertaking; she was to decorate Lancaster House for the traditional banquet offered to the Sovereign, a few days after the Coronation, by the Secretary of State for Foreign Affairs.

At Lancaster House there could be no question of improvising. The setting was a grand eighteenth century mansion, newly done up and gleaming in white and gold; Constance had only to ask and treasures from the Victoria and Albert and the Wellington Museum at Apsley House were put at her disposal. But the flowers had to be correspondingly formal, and she has described in *Party Flowers* how her florists made 'Grinling Gibbons' drops of fruit and flowers to hang round the walls, and tiny 'flames' of flowers to take the place of real flames in the gold candelabra.

Meanwhile, the firm's ordinary work had more than doubled. Regular clients wanted special effects for the Coronation parties and their window-boxes. An appeal was sent out to all the old hands, and they left husbands and children and came trooping back, delighted to be in harness again and to have their share in Constance's great hour. Robbo remembers worrying lest the reigning staff should resent the intrusion of old timers, but her fears were groundless. The magnitude of the task ahead ensured that once more, Constance would work everybody into the ground.

The sheer organizational effort required a steady business head, and one not distracted by purely floral concerns. It was a great joy to Constance that her son Anthony Marr was persuaded to abandon his career in broadcasting and to join the firm, of which he is chairman today.

The pace hotted up through May – though this did not keep Constance from having her usual display at Chelsea Show. Each week, as the stands went up along the route, the team from the Ministry toured it – Sir Eric de Normann, the Permanent Secretary, Major Hobkirk, the Bailiff of the Royal Parks, Mr Bedford, Mr Hepburn, and Constance. They could now visualize more clearly where the flowers would go and how many would be wanted. The three-deep line of scarlet geraniums at the Queen Victoria Memorial was too thin – there must be an addition to the shelf to widen the bank. The baskets swinging above the Duke of York's Steps were insufficiently lavish, there must be more ivy-leaved geraniums. The drifts of blue and white hydrangeas, interspersed with white stocks, on the Colonial Office stand were liable to block the view of those sitting immediately behind; Mr Bedford wanted them taken out of their pots and laid on their sides in peat; Mr Hepburn was unhappy about the watering problem this would cause. Doubts were felt about the stability of the huge container which was to hold the flowers at Hyde Park Corner. Mr Hepburn reported that owing to the hot weather, (ironic that it was a warm spring when the weather on the actual day was to be so chilly), plants were opening before their time; his stock of blue cinerarias would be much reduced. Mrs Spry suggested that any deficiencies could be filled in with common ponticum rhododendron, which would look beautiful if stripped of its leaves and massed. And so it went on.

To Rosemary Hume fell the infinitely complex job of planning the luncheon menu, suitable for guests from all over the world, some of whom would not be meat-eaters. Only the soup and the coffee could be hot, as there were no cooking facilities attached to the room. On 18 May she gave a lunch-party at the cookery school, to which were invited the Minister and the team, to taste the exact food proposed: consommé, cold trout with sauce verte, Chicken Elizabeth, the dish with a delicate curry-flavoured sauce which she had invented for the occasion, and which has since passed into the British housewife's repertory, and for sweets a choice of lemon soufflé, strawberry gâteau and chocolate roulades. It was all pronounced delicious.

The army of young waitresses were outfitted with their uniform, grey sprigged overall dresses designed for them by Victor Stiebel, tied with blue sashes, and adorned with a jewelled crown on blue moiré ribbon which was Constance's gift; the whole outfit was very pretty, and constituted a trophy which was proudly worn all summer. Effie Barker, a Berkshire neighbour and friend of Constance's who was to supply the lettuces for the luncheon from her farm, was informed that she would also be put in charge of the waiting. She protested that this was a skill quite beyond her. 'Nonsense,' she was told, 'you've been served by waiters all your life, of course you must know how it's done.'

The room received its drapes and tablecloths, and the end wall was filled by a magnificent tapestry, taking up the colours of red, blue and gold, which the Minister had unearthed from one of his stores. It was now ready for its red flowers. They arrived from San Remo on the Saturday morning, having been expected on the Friday, and the rosebuds were looking limp. Unpacked, the stems hammered, then immersed in pails of warm water and set in a cool place, they recovered miraculously. The anxiety then was, would they be too fully open before Tuesday morning? The gift was a superb one, totalling thousands of blooms, and Sunday morning was spent building it up into the huge wall groups and the circular table bouquets.

Meanwhile, the Commonwealth flowers had been flown in, and deposited in Hyde Park for the attention of Mr Hepburn and his staff. Privately, the Minister had decided that the Spry contingent should arrange them in the containers provided on the Commonwealth stands, since most of them were cut flowers, and this was, in his estimation, a job for flower decorators rather than for gardeners; but anticipating affront taken by the one party and long hours of overtime to be demanded from the other, he wisely held his hand. Fate played into it in a tragic manner he could never have foreseen.

When, around midday, nothing seemed to be happening in Parliament Square, Mr Eccles and Val Pirie got into a taxi and proceeded to Hyde Park, where they found that Hepburn had just died of a heart attack. The unfortunate man was a casualty of the Coronation. For weeks he had been worrying over the weather and the progress of his acres of plants, and getting up in the middle of the night to open or close with his own hands the ventilators in his greenhouses; he had literally worked himself to death.

There was no time to give the flowers a preliminary soaking, as had been done with the San Remo ones. The Minister directed that they should be brought immediately to the Square, and Val Pirie broke it to the team just finishing the luncheon room that another gigantic task lay before them, and appealed for volunteers. She got no refusals. An evening meal at an hotel was arranged for, and they worked through the evening and into the small hours.

It is this almost eerie experience that they remember best. Partly it was the strangeness and beauty of the flowers, the South African proteas particularly, and the many unfamiliar Indian blooms, but chiefly it was the exhilaration of working to an audience, instead of their usual routine of working behind the scenes. People had already begun to take up position for their two-night vigil on the pavements, others were touring the processional route, including parties of Commonwealth visitors who recognized their own flowers with cries of delight. The spectacle of these decorators at work was a most welcome distraction. They had become part of the show.

The Minister and his wife only left the Square but once, and then it was to return with a car-load of coffee and sausage rolls. Mrs Eccles' cook Florence, 'totally dedicated', had been making the sausage rolls all afternoon.

Somehow, by the light of arc-lamps, it was finished; and in spite of the haste and the impossibility of planning, they had contrived to make their blocks and drifts of colour, and to build up the strelitzias into huge, elegant fan-shapes. Then they got last or first trains and buses home, and snatched a few hours' sleep.

Next day, the groups in the retiring and luncheon rooms set up for the Royal Family in the Annexe were arranged, with a basket of Blanc Double de Coubert roses for the Queen's room: 'we hoped,' wrote Constance, 'that the sweetness, the simplicity of this lovely white rose might be found appropriate.' Effie Barker, coming up with a load of lettuce in her little farm van, found the van and herself commandeered by Constance. They toured the Parliament Square stands, with Constance standing up in the truck filling the flower vases from a watering can; it had always been a religion with her that cut flowers must not go thirsty. The sight delighted the by-now dense crowd, and she raised a succession of cheers.

She and Val Pirie spent the night in a room allotted to them in a Governmental hostel, within walking distance of the Abbey, and by five in the morning they were anxiously waiting outside the Annexe for an official to arrive with the key. The vases were given a last inspection. Then it was the turn of those in the luncheon room, while Rosemary Hume and her staff worked flat out to load the serving tables, and the young waitresses practised carrying their trays up a steep flight of steps and through a narrow door. Two television sets had been installed so that they could watch the ceremony, but except for the solemn moment of the actual crowning, no one had time to pause.

Then, the service ended, guests began to pour in from the Abbey. Constance has described it: 'The beauty and colour of the scene far exceeded anything we had imagined. The room gleamed and glimmered like a jewel-encrusted tapestry.' Everyone remembers some special figure; in George Foss's case it was a woman in a dress of oyster satin covered in rose-coloured diamonds. Constance's cast had assembled, and gloriously peopled her stage.

And she and the Minister had the gratification of hearing praise on all sides; not only for the delicious and imaginative food (so different, one may make bold to say, from anything that would have been provided by the costliest hotel), but for the deft young Hebes in their grey frocks and blue sashes. 'Mais qui sont toutes ces jolies mees?' enquired one potentate whose second language was French; and on its being explained to him that they were students, from good families, turned waitress in order to do honour to the Queen, he concluded regretfully: 'Ah! – alors elles ne seront pas libres ce soir.'

When it was all over, there remained platefuls of the exquisitely fine brown bread and butter which had accompanied the ham cornets. Inspiration descended upon George Foss; he had it piled on to trays, and carried out to the patient and famished crowd; a crowd by this time chilled and damp also. But if the Coronation weather was unkind, it did at least ensure that Constance's 'talent for perishable splendour' was not so perishable as all that. The flowers remained fresh for many days, and gave pleasure to thousands more, while the red bouquets of the luncheon did a further spell of duty in London hospitals.

Next day, the Coronation Honours List included a K C V O for the Minister, and an O B E for Constance. Letters of congratulation poured in, but those which gave her most pleasure were from her colleagues of the Ministry team, the very people who had cold-shouldered her a year before.

But there could be no letting up. The flowers for the Lancaster House banquet (they did not do the food) absorbed all their energies for the rest of the week. As described by Constance in *Party Flowers,* it sounds more like a florist's than a decorator's occasion, but in fact there were superb groups of white, cream and golden flowers, most of them a gift from Covent Garden, in the reception rooms, and there was the filling of two nine-foot-high malachite vases, presented by the Czar to Queen Victoria, which had been placed one each side of the great staircase. Some of the larger exotics from the Commonwealth gift had been set aside, and they were supplemented by hippeastrums, eremurus, and huge foliages presented by the Palm House at Kew. George Foss stood on a ladder to fix them, and the completed groups stood seventeen feet; gilt chairs placed beneath them looked like dolls' furniture in comparison. 'But we ought to have borrowed a couple of guardsmen,' says George Foss regretfully, 'to give a real sense of scale.'

Later that year, Constance attended an Investiture. There were those who thought that 'Dame Constance' was a title which would fittingly have recognized all she had done, but there were many services to be rewarded, and after all, she had made her own fame.

She herself had never expected to receive any mark of royal favour. She went to the Palace in a state of high emotion, and when her son and Daphne Holden, who had accompanied her, looked for her at the end of the ceremony, she was nowhere to be found. Overwhelmed, she had run out of the Palace, got into a taxi, and driven straight back to the shop.

10. LAST YEARS

Constance was sixty-six at the time of the Coronation, and she had eight more years to live. Her vitality was as intense as ever. In September of Coronation year she was off to Norway to lecture on flower arrangement to groups of NATO wives, and she continued to be in enormous demand as a lecturer at home. The nervous strain of these talks increased, and before them she would clutch the demonstrator's hand or demand an arm to help her up on to the platform, but once she rose to speak, all the nervousness fell away.

Sometimes in these later years there would be mild heckling, largely owing to the excesses of the flower-club movement, for which she was held responsible. She enjoyed these tussles, and dealt with them as cheerfully as she had handled the obstreperous parents of Homerton. 'You shall have your turn later,' she would tell the objector, and when the lecture was ended – 'now then, you, let battle commence.' He – it was usually a man – would then most likely find that he and Mrs Spry were of one mind.

She was equally active as a writer. Two short books, *Party Flowers*, embodying the Coronation experiences, and *Simple Flowers,* which stresses the 'everywoman' element in her thinking, came out in 1955 and 1957 respectively. Her publication for 1956 was on a massive scale, *The Constance Spry Cookery Book*, in which she collaborated with Rosemary Hume.

The idea of doing it was Constance's, inspired partly by the interest which the Coronation lunch had aroused, and every word of it was written by her, mostly on her so-called holidays at Ard Daraich. But it is not her book in the sense that *Come*

Into the Garden, Cook was. That was an amateur's book, and this is a professional's; the actual recipes and expertise are Rosemary Hume's. Constance is careful to explain in her introduction that she is to be regarded as 'Rosemary's stooge', who watched, and copied, and queried, and demanded fuller explanations of processes which the expert might take for granted.

The title was insisted upon by the publisher, Constance's being the famous name, and it worried her that this was, in effect, an injustice to Miss Hume. Like many injustices it has had a boomerang effect. The book had a success which startled both collaborators; it was the first important cookery book since the war, the first to challenge the worthy but rather stodgy reign of 'Mrs Beeton'; despite many subsequent competitors it holds it place today. As a result, Constance is 'the cookery woman' to a great many of the younger generation, who have been given the book as a wedding present, and the real nature of her achievement is forgotten.

But in truth, food was with her an interest second only to flowers; through them both she reached out to the art of living. 'The kitchen should be raised to the status of a studio', she says in her preamble; that this has largely happened is due in no small measure to the charm and glamour with which she invests work which had previously been regarded as humdrum. The book is as readable as a novel. She recalls her childhood delight in fruits and savours, her culinary struggles as a bride (distance lending enchantment to that particular view), but unlike most epicures, she is not interested in wine, except as an ingredient of cookery. She herself never felt the need of alcoholic stimulus, and while her guests would be served with exquisitely appropriate wines, she would shamefacedly be sipping a fruit juice. In the little hostess book which she wrote with the Winkfield students in mind, and which was published posthumously, the chapter on wine is contributed by her son.

The last of her flower books was *Favourite Flowers*, published in 1959, and if, after such a shelf-full, she had seemed to repeat herself, it would not have been surprising, On the contrary, this is her best piece of writing, easy, graceful, the snatches of poetry which continually bubbled through her mind gaily integrated into the text, the excitement of new discovery communicating itself as vividly as ever, and the descriptions of individual plants and flowers done with a fastidious choice of words that can compare with Colette's. 'Regarde, Maurice!' continually exclaimed the novelist to her husband as she lay dying; similarly, Constance bids us look and look and never let the eye grow stale.

The new colours evolved by rose hybridists in the 'fifties, grey, and mauve, and café-au-lait (merely, it is to be feared, regarded as steps on the way to the hoped-for blue rose), enchant her and she devotes a chapter to them. Alas, their constitution proved as poor as their popular appeal, and most of them vanished from commerce as rapidly as they had arrived. Today, the turkey-red and fishpaste-pink roses triumph at Chelsea, and almost the only stand on which you will see roses in 'grisaille and gold' is that of Constance Spry.

Her dislike of travel in all forms had never been allowed to interfere with her relish for new scenes, or with the spreading of the flower-arrangement gospel, and when she was invited to undertake an Australian lecture tour in the spring of 1959 she had no thought of refusing, though her friends did question whether a woman in her seventies should pack so much activity into a short space. Her phobia about doctors and illness was as intense as ever, and she would not hear of having a medical check-up. The sick had her sympathy, flowers and presents, but were kept out of her sight; death as a subject was absolutely taboo.

Sheila Macqueen was prevailed on to leave husband and children for a spell, and accompany her as demonstrator. They sailed on the P. & O. *Himalaya* early in February, and stopped off for a day at Colombo, where Constance gave a talk and did a round of sightseeing. In the evening she was alarmingly exhausted. Sheila Macqueen was perturbed, and wrote home: 'I shall have to be more firm,' but being firm with Constance was not easy, she resented any idea of being supervised or checked. She recovered on board ship, and seemed in excellent health and spirits for the rest of the tour.

There was a reception by the Mayor at Perth, and a talk; then on by boat to Melbourne for several lectures; then by train to Sydney, for she still steadfastly refused to fly. The guard on the train proved a passionate gardener, and they talked orchids half the night.

A large-scale opening in Sydney brought on the usual agonies of nerves, followed by the usual triumph; then north to Brisbane, then back to Sydney, then Adelaide; everywhere two lectures a day to packed audiences; 'she went to town more than I have ever heard her,' Sheila Macqueen wrote home. Sometimes her hosts were a trifle disappointed to find that she flagged on tours of their gardens, and would really rather sit swapping stories indoors; it probably did not occur to them that she was growing physically tired.

Summaries of her lectures in the Australian press show her still championing freedom of expression. 'Beware of stylizing. Accept no rules. Let the flowers remind you of how they looked when growing. You are not human unless you have a way of expressing yourself. Flowers are the contemporary woman's paint-box. I detest set arrangements such as a triangle of roses or a crescent moon of chrysanthemums. Don't make lovely flowers into statements of geometry.' One trusts the Australian ladies heeded her advice, and stopped their ears against the siren voices from America.

She was home in time for Chelsea, and a letter from the president of an Australian Garden Society expresses pleasure that she had done a 'Souvenir of Australia' arrangement on her stand, and informs her that following her visit flower arrangement goes on apace, new groups are constantly being formed and are exchanging material by air.

She soon had a further activity on her hands, for Roy Hay had succeeded in persuading the Royal Gardeners' Orphan Fund, of which he was chairman, that they needed a woman on the committee and that it should be Constance. The Fund's object, to give further education to young people who might otherwise not get the chance, was one dear to the heart of George Fletcher's daughter and Homerton's ex-headmistress, but she knew that she was no committee woman. 'That's all right,' Roy Hay told her over lunch, 'you need only attend one meeting, and after that just give us your blessing.' In the event she gave much more, for she let it be known that she would lecture without fee to any flower or garden club which was willing to pass round the hat. In this way she raised more than a thousand pounds for the Fund in the last year of her life.

Constance's American friend, Helen Kirkpatrick, now Mrs Robbins Milbank, had not been in England for five years, but she suddenly had a strong feeling that it was important her husband should meet Constance, and they came over that summer. They found her in excellent form at Winkfield, and when the new Mrs Milbank confessed that she had been attending an Ikebana class, she was told: 'If I catch you doing any of those affected designs, my girl, I'll cut you off without a farthing.' The party went north, and had glorious weather at Ard Daraich. 'Constance did seem to be very much preoccupied with tidying things up, handing the shop over to Tony, getting papers into order, etc., but then she was nearly seventy, and retirement of some degree seemed eminently sensible, albeit unlike her,' Mrs Milbank recalls. (In fact Constance was seventy-three, but she had always been cagey about revealing her age; it is one of her few Edwardian traits.)

She was as buoyantly inventive over the 'Christmas non-sense, as ever, and on the evening of 3 January, as they sat round the dinner-table at Winkfield, she was full of ideas for the Christmas of 1960. Going upstairs to her drawing-room after dinner, she suddenly stumbled, and lost consciousness. She was carried to her bed, and an hour later, she was dead.

It was the sort of end we must all hope for, and to one who had so greatly dreaded illness and death, it was particularly merciful. Nevertheless, the utterly unexpected nature of her going inflicted a profound shock on her circle; some of them took two years fully to recover. She had been so much the mainspring of everything they did that at first it seemed impossible to carry on without her.

Of course it was not; and the best memorial they could give her was to continue all her activities in her tradition, but kept, as indeed it always had been, flexible and attuned to the changing times. Anthony Marr headed the whole business and the shops – by the time of Constance's death there were three, two in London and one at Guildford. Rosemary Hume continued the cookery school, and Winkfield went on under the joint headship of herself and Christine Dickie. Harold Piercy, a brilliant young recruit at the time of the Coronation, became head of the flower school; George Foss and Sheila Macqueen were the principal lecturers. And Val Pirie devoted herself to the care of the shattered and desolate Shav Spry; she married him in 1962.

The tributes which poured in proved, if proof were needed, that Constance was known and loved all over the world, and the flowers at her funeral were like royalty's – chiefly white, because everyone remembered how she loved white. But on a bitter January day the effect was strangely cold and bleak, 'not a bit like Constance,' the mourners said afterwards, remembering that she had always been warm and gay. They were also invited to contribute to the Royal Gardeners' Orphan Fund, and did so to the tune of £900; after which it was decided to set up a special Constance Spry Fund in her memory, as an independent charity operating in collaboration with the RGOF. The flower clubs of the country have supported it loyally ever since.

No doubt the world expected Constance Spry to die rich, but she died no more than moderately prosperous; her will left a little over £27,000. She had never really been interested in making money; she did what she could to promote the prosperity of floristry as a trade, but it mattered more to her to help raise the general standard of the work. The nurserymen and the seedsmen benefited more by her writing and lecturing, of which the constant theme was that people should grow, and should arrange, for themselves. And this is what we continue to do.

A recent survey showed that we in Britain spend on cut flowers and pot plants only half as much per head of the population as the French, a quarter as much as the Germans and Norwegians, a sixth as much as the Danes.* Yet no one would deny our claim to be the leading gardeners, flower lovers and flower arrangers of the world.

Her influence on the standards of professional floristry has

* *The Marketing of Flowers in the United Kingdom.* Wye College, 1971.

of course been revolutionary. There is still some ugly work being done, and will be as long as there is a demand for it, but the general improvement in taste gives scope to hundreds of florists, many of them Spry-trained, who can claim the status of artists. The nature of the work they do has altered with the times. People live in smaller houses, and the few who still employ a professional to do their flowers regularly require smaller groups, but even wealthy women now mostly arrange these themselves. The flower decorator is chiefly called in for weddings and big functions, when the groups will still be on the magnificently lavish Spry scale.

But it is in the homes of ordinary people, some of them as humble as the one she was born in, that Constance's influence is most precious, and this whether they have heard of her or not. Primarily through flowers, but also in her whole approach to living, she has set free the artist in countless women and a good many men who before her day had no means of creating beauty. It often seems now that we live in a world of increasing violence and destruction, but it is forgotten how much more scope there also is for the opposite qualities, those Constance stood for, creativeness and peace.

And even those who can't share in this act of creation can see its effects around them, where there was little or none before; in the church or chapel, in the hospital ward or waiting-room, in the public library, at the flower festival for which they will queue as though it were a football match. I have never felt myself closer to Constance than in Salisbury Cathedral, the week after Easter, when the decorations were still in place. Great golden stars of flowers gleamed here and there at the foot of the pillars, enhancing the majesty of the nave; most of them just the ordinary flowers of spring, forsythia and cat-kins and daffodils, but placed by the hands of artists, and all done for love.

Truly, the good this woman did lives after her.

APPENDIX

Constance Spry's Principal Publications

(The publishers in every case are J. M. Dent & Sons.)

1934 *Flower Decoration*
1937 *Flowers in House and Garden*
1940 *A Garden Notebook*
1942 *Come Into the Garden, Cook*
1951 *Summer and Autumn Flowers*
1951 *Winter and Spring Flowers*
1953 *How to Do the Flowers*
1955 *Party Flowers*
1956 *The Constance Spry Cookery Book*
        (with Rosemary Hume)
1957 *Simple Flowers*
1959 *Favourite Flowers*

INDEX